Windows 10

Great Guide To Windows 10

By Annabel Jacobs

SECTIONS

 Section 1 | Getting Windows 10

 Section 2 | Getting Started

 Section 3 | Personalization | Make it yours

 Section 4 | File Management & Search

 Section 5 | Working with Apps

 Section 6 | System & User Management

CHAPTERS

Section 1| Getting Windows 10

Chapter 01 Understanding the User Accounts   14

Chapter 02 Installing / Upgrading & Setting Up Windows   16

Section 2| Getting Started

Chapter 03 Getting Around the Interface   23

Chapter 04 Getting the Basic Things Done   33

Section 3| Personalization| Make it yours

Chapter 05 Essential Customization   55

Section 4| File Management & Search

Chapter 06 Understanding Files, Folders &Drives   78

Chapter 07 Using the File Explorer   82

Chapter 08 Common Files& Folder Operations   96

Chapter 09 Managing Files   110

Chapter 10 Searching with Cortana   121

Section 5| Working with apps

Chapter 11 The Mail app   135

Chapter 12 Working with Calendar app   149

Chapter 13 Working with People app   161

Chapter 14 Windows 10 apps Round up   169

Chapter 15 Managing Apps   175

Section 6| System & User Management

Chapter 16 Administrator & User Account Management   184

Chapter *17*: Securing your system with Windows Defender   186

Chapter *18* Backup & Restore   206

TABLE OF CONTENTS

Section 1| Getting Windows 10

Chapter 01 Understanding the User Accounts   14

    What is a User Account?   14

    Types of Accounts   15

      Local account vs. Microsoft Account   15

Chapter 02 Installing / Upgrading & Setting Up Windows   16

    Upgrading to Windows   16

    Setting up Window 10 on a New System   19

    Windows 10, First Run   20

Section 2| Getting Started

Chapter 03 Getting Around the Interface   23

    The Desktop   23

    The Task Bar   24

    The Action Center   25

    The Start Menu   29

Chapter 04 Getting the Basic Things Done   33

    Launching Apps   33

    Multitasking   35

      Maximizing, Minimizing apps & Quitting apps   38

      Quick Access Desktop   39

    Task View   **Error! Bookmark not defined.**

    Working with Virtual Desktops   40

      Creating Virtual Desktop   40

      Manage Apps between Virtual Desktops   42

Switch between virtual Desktops   45

Close a Desktop   46

Pinning and Unpinning apps   46

Adding shortcuts to Desktop   49

Enter& Exit Tablet Mode   50

Locking your PC   52

Sleep, Login, Restart & Shutdown   53

Section 3| Personalization| Make it yours

Chapter 05 Essential Customization   55

Customizing Desktop   56

Desktop Background& Color   56

Screen Resolution   59

Lock Screen   62

Customizing Action Center   64

Customizing Quick Actions   64

Customizing Notifications   65

Action Center Display   66

Quiet Hours   68

Customizing Start Menu   69

Customizing the Left Pane   69

Pinning & Moving Tiles   71

Creating & Naming Groups of Tiles   72

Unpin Tiles   72

Resizing Tiles   72

Turning Live On/Off   73

Switch to Start Screen   73

Customizing Task Bar   74

Auto-Hide Task Bar   74

Customizing System Tray icons   75

Automatic Sleep Time   76

Section 4| File Management & Search

Chapter 06 Understanding Files, Folders &Drives   78

  Various Elements of Windows Filing System   78

    What is a file?   78

    What is a folder?   79

    Where are the files stored?   80

    What are Libraries?   80

    Windows Folder Structure   80

Chapter 07 Using the File Explorer   82

  Launching File Explorer   82

  File Explorer Interface   83

    Ribbon Menu   85

    Pinning Ribbon Menu   86

  Using the File Explorer to Navigate   87

    Where is my data?   87

    Navigating Windows Filing Structure   88

  Quick Access   90

    Pinning/Unpinning folders to Quick Access   91

  Sharing Files from File Explorer   92

  Introducing One Drive   94

    What is OneDrive?   94

    Launching & Adding Files to OneDrive   94

    Synchronizing Files   95

Chapter 08 Common Files & Folder Operations   96

  Create new Folder   96

  Moving File/Folders with File Explorer   97

    Moving multiple files/folders   98

  Copy Folders through File Explorer   103

  Renaming Folder   104

  Delete & Restore Files   105

Permanently Delete Files/Folders   105

Restoring File   106

Zipping/Unzipping Folders   106

Pinning Folders to Start Menu   108

Chapter 09 Managing Files   110

Customizing File Explorer   110

Changing View   110

Adding Columns   112

Customizing Panes   113

Resizing the Navigation Pane   113

Hiding Navigation Pane   114

Preview Pane   115

Showing Libraries   116

Sorting and Grouping Files/Folders   116

Show/Hide File Extension   120

Chapter 10 Searching with Cortana   121

What is Cortana?   121

Setting up Cortana   122

The Interface   122

Personalizing Cortana   123

Adding/Removing Interests   123

Adding favorite locations   125

Cleaning Memory   127

Setting Reminders in Cortana   127

Accessing Upcoming Reminders   128

Accessing Reminders from past   129

Searching with Cortana   130

Searching the PC   130

Searching the web   133

Natural language Commands   133

Section 5 | Working with apps

Chapter 11 The Mail app   135

  Accounts Set up for Mail, People and Calendar   136

  Setting up Mail app   137

  Mail app Basics   141

    Switching Accounts   141

    Composing Emails   141

    Attaching Files   142

    Adding Multiple Recipients   143

    Sending Email   144

    Read, Reply & Forward   144

    Flagging Emails   145

    Going Back   146

    Changing Signature   146

  Managing Accounts Settings   147

    How to Conserve Data?   148

    Adding Email Accounts   148

Chapter 12 Working with Calendar app   149

  Calendar View & Settings   152

    Hiding/Showing Calendar   152

    Changing Color for a Calendar   154

    Changing View   154

    Setting Work Week and Working Hours   156

  Basics of the Calendar app   157

    Viewing Appointments   157

    Creating Appointment   157

    Adding Detail   158

Chapter 13 Working with People app   161

  Filtering Contacts   161

  Adding Contact   163

Edit Card 166

Changing Account for Saving contact 166

Deleting contact 166

Sharing Contact Card 167

Sending email from People app 168

Chapter 14 Windows 10 apps Round up 169

Apps for browsing the internet 170

Internet Explorer **Error! Bookmark not defined.**

Other apps 173

Chapter 15 Managing Apps 175

Installing apps from App Store 175

Uninstalling apps 178

Apps Memory Usage 180

App Permission 181

Restricting an App 182

Section 6| System & User Managemen

Chapter 16 Administrator & User Account Management 184

Managing Administrator Account 185

Adding image to your Account 185

Verifying your Identity 186

Changing PIN 187

Removing PIN 188

Changing Account Type 189

Changing Password 190

Managing MultiUser Accounts 191

Windows 10 Family Feature 191

Setting up Multiple Accounts 192

Creating a Microsoft Account 192

Creating Local Account 194

Setting up Family Features 196

Removing Accounts   197

Chapter 17 Securing your System with Windows Defender   186

Scan & Notifications   199

Windows Defender Settings   201

Manual Scan   202

Viewing and Removing Detected Files   203

Updates   204

Chapter 18 Backup & Restore   206

Windows 10 Backup Tools   206

Backup & Restore Windows 7   207

Restoring your Backup   209

Reset Windows   210

	Notes & Tips
	Notes for Users who have upgraded from Windows 7 & 8
	Definitions of common terminologies for beginners & Common Questions
	Keyboard Shortcuts
	Notes for touch device users

① SECTION
GETTING WINDOWS 10

Chapter 01

UNDERSTANDING THE USER ACCOUNTS

What is a User Account?

Like its predecessor, Windows 10 is a multi-user operating system. With individual User Accounts, each individual user can keep files and system preferences separate from all other users. Conversely, you may say that your computer identifies you with your User Account. You use a combination of a username and password to login to your account.

A User Account is important for three major reasons:

1- **Security**: User Accounts prevent unauthorized access to your PC.
2- **Multiple User Profiles**: If you are sharing your PC with other users, User Accounts save profiles for individual users. In this way every user can login using their own specific account details and maintain personal desktop preferences, browser favorites, desktop shortcuts and files on the same PC.
3- **Controlled Access**: You can control the access of individuals to your PC by settings up different User Accounts and granting them different privileges. For example as a parent you can set up account for your child and restrict the account from downloading any software or changing system files.

Before we start with the Windows 10 installation/upgradation it's important to understand different types of User Accounts in Windows 10 and decide which type of User Account you will use to log in to your operating system; as this information is required during the installation process.

Types of Accounts

With Windows 10, you have the ability to create user profile with your Microsoft account, besides traditional local accounts.

1- **Microsoft Account:** Microsoft account is your account associated to any of the Microsoft services. If you have a Hotmail, Outlook, Live, MSN email, Xbox Live or Office 365 account, you already have a Microsoft account. If you do not have a Microsoft account you can set up a Microsoft account online for free. Your Microsoft account will give you an identity with all Microsoft Online services and access to Outlook.com email and OneDrive - a free cloud storage tool by Microsoft. You can also create a Microsoft account during installation process of Windows 10.

2- **Local Account:** If you are using PC for a while, every time you log in your PC you are in fact using a *local account*. A local account gives you access to the PC however it has no connection with Microsoft; neither does it identify you with Microsoft online services. For example you cannot use your local account to sign-in to your Outlook email.

 Remember that a Microsoft Account is *required* to purchase apps from Microsoft App Store. Also you will need a Microsoft account to access and use certain features a few bundled apps in Windows 10.

Local account vs. Microsoft Account

If you opt to use a Microsoft account type, you will be able to:

✓ Synchronize your settings across multiple devices (laptops, phone and tablets etc.)
✓ Synchronize system preferences, web browser settings, saved passwords, language preferences etc. All personalized settings will go with you.
✓ One time sign-in: Once you are signed in with your Microsoft account you will not need to sign in again for associated Microsoft services such as OneDrive, Skype, Outlook etc.
✓ Make purchase in Windows 10 App Store

 Microsoft recommends using Microsoft Online account (preferably) for personal/individual use as with Microsoft account you can leverage with the full functionalities of bundled apps such as Mail, Calendar, iCloud, People etc.

While using a Microsoft account may sound as a viable option, it may not always be the best suited choice. For instance, when setting up public workstations to be used in schools or in a workplace, you may opt for simpler local accounts. You may also opt for a local account if you do not want your computer to be limited only with the identity of one person, and desire a certain level of anonymity. With local accounts you will still be:

- ✓ Able to access and fully use your Windows 10 PC
- ✓ Download, Install and run software which did not surface from the Windows Apps Store, such as Google's Chrome or Mozilla's Firefox or Adobe's Photoshop.
- ✓ All your system settings will be saved securely on one workstation.

Chapter 02
INSTALLING / UPGRADING & SETTING UP WINDOWS

Upgrading to Windows

Anyone with an acceptable device can upgrade to Windows 10 for free, with free support from Microsoft, including updates and other software for the lifetime of the device. If you are upgrading from Windows 7, you need to verify system requirements as follows:

Processor: 1 gigahertz (GHz) or faster.
RAM: 1 gigabyte (GB) (32-bit) or 2 GB (64-bit)
Free hard disk space: 16 GB.

To upgrade to Windows 10, follow these steps:

1- Identify the upgrade message pop-up in the system tray. Alternatively you can use the following link to Microsoft website to download your free upgrade. At the time of writing this book, the upgrade is available to individuals who have reserve their free upgrade. https://www.microsoft.com/en-us/windows/windows-10-upgrade
2- Click on the notification. This will pop up a window and walk you through Windows 10 features. Windows 10 will immediately start to download.
3- Once downloaded, follow the steps to successfully install it on your PC.

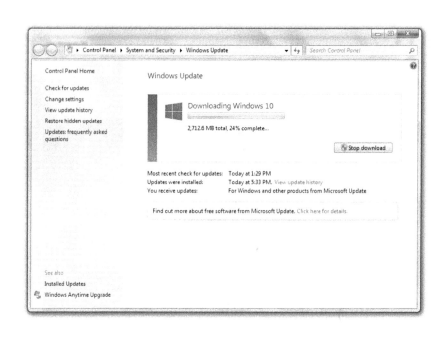

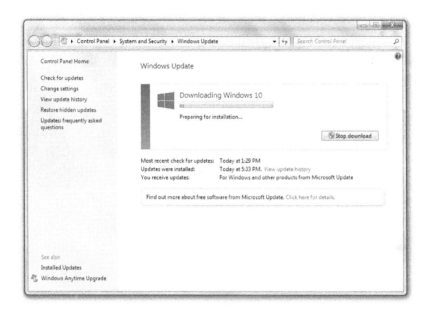

Setting up Window 10 on a New System

Windows XP and Windows Vista users will have to clean install Windows 10. Also, if you are making a computer from separate parts or wish to install Windows on Mac (with the Apple's built-in Bootcamp) you will need to install a fresh copy of Windows 10. While upgrading is free, purchasing a fresh copy will cost you $ 119.99. When purchasing a fresh copy of Windows 10, you have the following options:

1- **Buy a USB installed drive**. You may purchase a Windows 10 USB drive from a nearby computer & electronics retailer, or from the Microsoft online store. In latter case, Microsoft will ship (in a few days) a physical drive which you can connect to your computer and install Windows 10 from it.
2- **Buy downloadable copy**: You may purchase a downloadable copy and create your own USB/DVD Drive.
3- Purchase installed DVD (from retailers such as Amazon)

Whether you have created your own USB drive from the downloadable Windows 10 copy, or purchased a Windows 10 USB, you will have a set-up file provided in the USB. Simply run the set-up and follow the instructions as they prompt. During the installation process you will be asked if you want to keep the software applications and files on the new installation or if you want to clean install.

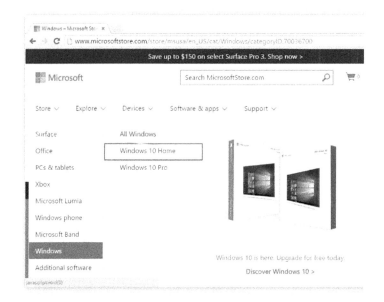

To purchase Windows 10 USB Drive go to Microsoft Store -> Windows -> Windows 10 Home

 If you are setting up Window 10 for the first time, signing in with your Microsoft account can give you a significant jump start by synchronizing settings

Windows 10, First Run

When you first start your Windows 10 machine, you will have to set up a few things such as country, language and time zone. These preferences are already set for you if you are upgrading your operating system. During the setup process you will be prompted to:

1- Connect to a wireless network. Choose your wireless network and provide the password for authentication.
2- Choose **Express Settings** or **Customize settings** for installation. Microsoft recommends Express settings.
3- **Owner of the PC**: Specify the device owner; if the device belongs to an individual or is associated to an organization
4- **Set up a login account**: As discussed previously, during the installation process you will be asked choose the type of account (local account or Microsoft account) you would like to use

for logging in your computer. If you do not already have a Microsoft account and wish to use one, Microsoft prompts users to create an account during the installation process.

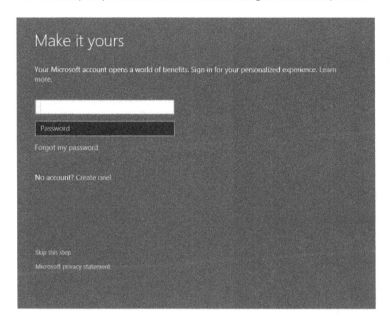

From the above figure:
- **Use a Microsoft Account**: Fill in the credentials in the text fields provided and click **Next**.
- **Create New Account**: Choose "No Account? Create One!" to create a new Microsoft account. Microsoft creates a new account and signs you in with it.
- **Use a local account:** Set up a local account by clicking on "**Skip this Step**" on the bottom left.

5- Setting up a Pin: If you choose to use your Microsoft account for your login, you will be prompted to set up a PIN. With the PIN set up you can login to your PC without having to type in your Microsoft account password. This feature is particularly handy if you are using Windows 10 on a tablet or touch device as typing a 4 figure code is much less of a hassle than typing a lengthy password on a touch screen. You may choose to skip setting up the PIN by clicking on Skip this step.

Remember a PIN only works with a device you set i.e. PIN works Locally.
PIN also helps protect your Microsoft account password.

2 SECTION
GETTING STARTED

Chapter 3
GETTING AROUND THE INTERFACE

The Desktop

As you successfully log into your account, you arrive on your desktop. The desktop is your starting point. In Windows 10, when you launch an app, it opens *inside* a window directly *on* the desktop and the app operation is consistent, irrespective of the type of app you are running. You can think of the desktop as an empty screen which holds one or more windows for every app you are working with.

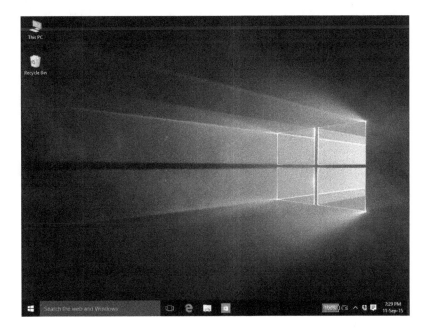

If you have upgraded from Windows 8, you will be pleased to find the traditional desktop and Start Menu have returned in Windows 10.

Apps for Windows 8 did not have the traditional close button. If you leave the app and jump to another screen, Windows either suspended the app or has sent it to background, depending on the apps design. However, now in Windows 10, apps have a close button and open on the desktop.

When you run Windows 10 for the first time you will be greeted with a desktop with a deep blue customizable background (as seen from the above figure). The desktop contains a single icon for the Recycle Bin. As the desktop is the most readily available destination on your PC, you might want to add shortcuts of your most frequently used apps or folders, or save files to the desktop. We will discuss adding shortcuts to the desktop in chapter 4 and customizing the desktop background in chapter 5.

Windows 10 introduces **Multiple Desktops**. You can regard each desktop as a virtual space containing its own apps. This is particularly helpful when you are multitasking between apps and working on different projects. In such a situations you may use different desktops for different projects with each desktop containing project specific apps. We will revisit multiple desktops in chapter 4.

The Task Bar and Start Menu are part of your desktop.

The Task Bar

Along the bottom of the screen you will find the Task Bar. The Task Bar houses the following elements:

- **Start Button**: On the far left you will find a button with a Windows icon. This is the Start button. The start button opens a vertical menu called the Start Menu. We will discuss the Start Menu in more detail later in this chapter.

- **Search Field**: Beside the Start button, lays a search field. You can use this search field to fetch files from your PC or to search the internet. **Cortana**, the built-in voice enabled virtual assistant lives in this search field. Chapter 10 discusses Cortana's searching features in detail.

- **Task View Icon**: Task View enables you to efficiently multitask between applications. From the Task View, you can open multiple desktops and sort applications to different desktops. Multitasking and virtual desktops are discussed in detail in chapter 4.

- **Apps**: On the center of the Task Bar you will find icons for apps, which are either pinned to the Task Bar, or are currently running on your PC.

Pinned Apps

Running Apps are indicated with blue bar under the App icon.

- **System Tray:** The system tray displays icons from applications which are running in the background. The system tray also displays the calendar entries and System Icons such as icons for volume control, internet connection, cloud storage etc.

The Task Bar is always available to the user even while running apps (contrary to the desktop which hides behind the app window). The only exception is when the user opts to run the app in full-screen; in that case the app window occupies the full screen and hides the Task Bar.

The Action Center

Microsoft with Windows 10 aims to provide a unified operating system to both desktop and touch-device users. The Action Center, is a new feature introduced in Windows 10 that specifically relates to the computing requirements of mobile device users, providing quick access to commonly used system settings. Besides, Action Center has a plethora of information which can be reached by simply tapping/clicking on the icon in system tray.

Users who have upgraded from Windows 8 will no longer find the **Charms bar**. However, you will be pleased to find that all the goodies from the Charms bar have been integrated into the **Action Center** without the annoyance of the difficult user interface.

To access the Action Center, identify the button on the far left of the system tray on Task Bar. As you click on the button, the Action Center will open in a full-length vertical panel spanning the left side of the desktop. The Action Center can be accessed anytime from the system tray.

To access the Action Center on touch devices, swipe from the right side of the screen.

Action Center provides a single place to:

- **View and manage notifications:** Action Center persistently notifies the user with system and app events such as: pending upgrades, calendar reminders, malware notification, mail and other apps. Notifications are generally categorized according to date.
- **Quick Actions**: On the bottom of the Action Center, locate four buttons (shaped like square tiles). Each button is a shortcut to common system settings such as screen brightness, volume control, Wi-Fi, Bluetooth etc. These Quick access buttons/tiles do not appear or disappear depending upon the device in use. Click on Expand to view more setting tiles. The active tiles are colored (according to your theme).

  Both notifications and quick access setting are customizable. We will revisit Action Center in chapter 5 when we discuss customization.

 Notifications

 Quick Actions

You can click on any notification and Action Center will open the associated app where you can take appropriate action. You may also take the following action for notifications, in the Action Center

View Notification: You can view detailed notifications by clicking on the small arrow on the top-right corner of the notification. Toggle the arrow to expand/collapse notifications to view notification details.

Clear Notification: You may also dismiss individual notifications by clicking on the small cross on the top-right corner which appears when you point to the notification. You can also dismiss groups of notifications by pointing on the group title and clicking on the small cross on the right. To clear all notifications in the Action Center, click on the ***Clear All*** button on the top-right.

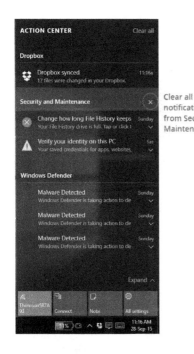

Clear all notifications from Security Maintenance

Dismiss all notificati

Dismiss Notifica

View Details

 Pop-up notifications slide in from the bottom left side of the screen; as opposed to the top-left.

The Start Menu

The Start Menu is your doorway to all of the programs, settings, files and functions on your system. The Start Menu is a hallmark of Windows and has been an integral part of Microsoft OS designs, since Windows 95.The vertical menu appears on the right side of the screen and can be accessed by clicking on the small button with the Windows Logo on the far left of the Task Bar. ▦ Alternatively, you may press the button with the Windows logo on your keyboard.

The Start Menu in Windows 10 has two independent panels:

1- **Fixed vertical menu:** The left side of the Start Menu gives you access to common functions like Power on, power off, settings, etc. Towards the top of the menu you will find the User Account with which you are logged in, followed by a list of frequently used apps. Depending upon how recently you have installed a specific app to your system, a list of recently installed apps will also show in the Start Menu. On the very bottom of the Start Menu you can find "**all apps**". When clicked, the left side of the menu will populate with the names of all the apps installed on your PC, and in alphabetic order.

2- **Resizable Panel with Live Tiles**: On the right side of the Start Menu you will find re-sizable tiles. You can hover the mouse along the right corner of the Start Menu and expand or squeeze the panel with the handle; the tiles will rearrange themselves within the grid accordingly. You are not able to switch off the tiles section completely. The tiles animate as you hover over them. Lives tiles will give you information about corresponding app at a glance. We will revisit the Start Menu and tiles section a number of times though this book to cover other important aspects of this built-in feature.

Fixed Vertical panel to access apps, Settings

Resizable Panel with Tiles

What are tiles?

Tiles are brightly colored square buttons. Every tile is perhaps a shortcut to your apps. When you click on a tile, the operating system opens the corresponding app. For example, clicking on Mail opens the Mail app. Unlike typical application shortcuts, tiles (*if set to live*) are capable of displaying information in real time. For example the weather app displays the weather information from the weather tile preview. You can get information at a glance i.e. without even having to launch the app. Similarly, the photo tile will display images from the gallery. Tiles also update over the internet to give important news headlines. Tiles are usually larger than typical shortcuts to facilitate users on touch devices.

The traditional Start Menu went missing in Windows 8 and was replaced by a start screen. Because the Start Menu was an integral part of Windows OS', since Windows 95, removing the Start Menu caused an uproar in the user community. Microsoft responded by bringing back the Start Menu in Windows 10. The Start Menu is now a hybrid version of the Start screen from Windows 8 and the traditional Start Menu. The new design is useful for users of different types of devices. Windows 10 users can still switch between the Start Menu and the full-fledge Start Screen. Search bar is no longer contained within Start Menu.

Chapter 04
GETTING THE BASIC THINGS DONE

With a basic understand of the user interface, we are in a good position to explore the operating system in more detail. This chapter details steps to accomplish every-day tasks.

Launching Apps

Apps lie at the heart of Windows 10. From watching a movie, browsing the internet, reading a book or checking email, you will find yourself using apps for every task you perform on your PC.

What are Apps? Desktop Programs& Windows Universal Apps?

Microsoft with Windows 8 and Windows 10 aims to provide a single operating system for mobile phones, tablets, notebooks and desktops. As the scope of this OS extends from traditional PCs to touch-devices, there comes a new class of software **apps** in addition to long-established programs (or Windows programs or Windows classic apps or Win32 executable apps).

The background

Apps (or applications) are small light-weight, highly task-oriented programs mostly optimized for touch screens. On the contrary desktop programs are full-fledged applications which are usually designed for use with a keyboard and mouse (such as Microsoft Excel, Adobe Photoshop etc.). Since Windows 8 was an OS for both tablets and notebooks, devices running Windows 8 were capable of running both Apps and desktop apps.

Until Windows 8 there has been speculation around apps terminology; initially called Metro Apps, and later renamed to Modern apps and then to Windows Store apps. However, now Microsoft has finally arrived to call them **"Windows Universal apps"** within Windows 10. Windows universal apps are apps which are coded once and can be used on different types of devices. Universal apps (extension .AppX) are distributed through the Windows Store and are available on all devices running Windows 10. Microsoft is urging developers to adopt the new standards of app development. Old legacy apps (or Windows executable apps) are still referred to as programs.

You can launch an App from the Task Bar and from the Start Menu.

Launching an app from the Start Menu

1- Click on the Start button to show the Start Menu.
2- Identify the **Most Used** section on the left panel. Click on any app to launch it.
3- If you cannot find the app you want to launch in the **Most Used** list, identify and click on the **All Apps** link on the bottom of the left panel. Find your desired app and click to launch.

Launching apps from Task Bar

To launch an app from the Task Bar simply click on the app icons in the Task Bar to launch it. If you have not pinned any apps to the Task Bar, then by default you only have icons for four apps, namely the Edge Browser, Windows Store and File Explorer. The number of apps accessible via the Task Bar may seem limited at first, however as you continue to use your PC, you will quickly identify a minimum number of the most frequently apps. You can pin those apps to the Task Bar and use the Task Bar to easily access them anytime. We will learn how to pin apps later in this chapter.

Multitasking

Most times you will want to work with multiple apps at a time: reading a book, listening to music and maybe even browsing the internet. Windows allows you to multitask i.e. launch, work with and switch between multiple apps at a time.

What is Multitasking?

Launching and working with multiple or more than one app at a time and jumping from one app to another is called multitasking. Operating systems which allow multitasking track the user's activity within each app and allow you to switch apps without losing data. For example let's say you are typing a document in Microsoft Word, and using Skype for IM. You can switch from Word to Skype and check for a new message and return to Word and continue right from where you left. You do not need to sign into Skype again or save and quit Microsoft Word before you switch to Skype. Most operating systems today allow users to multitask.

To understand multitasking in Windows 10, let's open multiple apps. I am launching Edge Browser, Twitter and the Calculator for this example. Notice:

- Each app opens in its own window.
- As you open apps, every app opens in a window above the previously opened app (depending upon your window size). From the figures below, notice that the Calculator lies on the top of Edge Browser and the Twitter app as it was launched lastly.

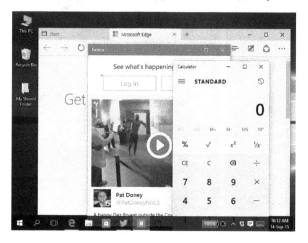

- As you open apps, the icon for each opened app will appear in the Task View. For this example you can see icons for Twitter & Calculator start to appear (in addition to the icon for Edge Browser which was already present).
- All the apps which are running are indicated by a *small blue bar* under the icon of the corresponding app. Identify blue bars under icons for Edge Browser, Twitter and Calculator

- The app on the top of the stack is the active app. The active app (or the app on which you are working) is always indicated with a lightly shaded square in Task Bar. In the figure above, the Calculator is the active app.

- You can switch between applications by clicking the icons of open apps from the Task Bar. In the figure below I have clicked on the Twitter app to bring it to the front of the stack. Now the Twitter app is the active app. Also notice that the Twitter icon is highlighted in the Task Bar.

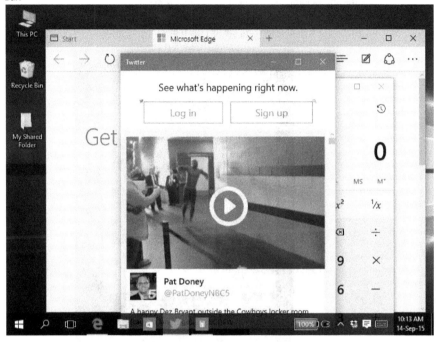

- Hover over the icon in the Task Bar to see a thumbnail preview of the app. The figure shows two Edge Browser windows have opened.
- You can see a thumbnail preview of all the applications you have opened in the Task View. We discuss Task View in detail, later in this section.

 You can switch between applications by using the following keyboard shortcut: **Alt+ Tab**.

While you are multitasking, you may need to hide the active window temporarily. If so, you can minimize the app window. Minimizing the app window will hide it from view, but it will still be running in the background. You can get back to the app anytime and continue working from where you left. To minimize an app window, identify the menu on the top right side of the app window.

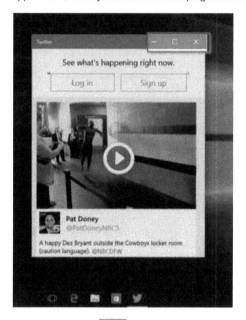

Click the small minus button on the very left to minimize the window. Notice in the Task Bar, the app icon is still visible and the blue bar under the icon indicates that the app is still running. You can show the app window again by clicking on its icon in the Task Bar.

If you wish that your app window stretches across the desktop screen so you have more workspace, then you can maximize the app window. To maximize the app window, simply click on the small square icon in the center of the top-right menu of the window. When working with a maximum sized window, the Maximize button toggles to the *resize* button. If you want to resize an app window click on the re-size button. The app window will shrink. When hovering your mouse along the edge of a window you will see re-size handles, which you can use to resize the app window.

To quit an app click on small cross icon beside the maximize icon.  This will kill the application. Depending upon the application you are working with you may need to save your work before you quit. You can also quit an app by:

1- Pointing to application's icon in the Task Bar to show its thumbnail preview
2- Move your mouse to the right-top corner of the preview and click the small "x" button as it appears.

Quick Access Desktop

If you are working with multiple apps and wish to minimize all app windows at a time to show the desktop, you can use the **show desktop** button. Identify a vertical button on the far right side of the system tray.

- **One click**: As you click on the button, all the app windows are immediately minimized showing the desktop.
- **Click Again**: You can bring all your app windows back into view by clicking on the vertical button again.
- **Hover**: If you hover on the vertical button you will be able to quick preview the desktop.

Task View

By now we have seen how to launch an application, minimize, maximize and quit applications and how to switch between open applications. There are times when you are working with more than just a few apps; let's say when you are planning for your vacation, writing an email to your client and doing some computation or intensive work with Microsoft Office tools. Your desktop can become cluttered very quickly. In such a situation Task View comes handy!

Task View is a brand new feature introduced in Windows 10. Task View takes multitasking to an advanced level. With Task View you can:

1- View all the open apps at a glance in a thumbnail preview. Manage apps by quitting unnecessary apps.
2- Create and manage multiple desktops. Task View enables you to have multiple desktops. Virtual desktops can be immensely helpful if you switch between projects while working. With multiple desktops you can open project/task specific apps in each desktop. You can open as many virtual desktops as per your work requirement. With virtual desktop, when

you need to switch between projects, you cans simply switch desktops instead of opening only relevant apps. In the next section we detail the steps you need to create and manage virtual desktops.

To launch Task View, click on the icon besides search field in Task Bar 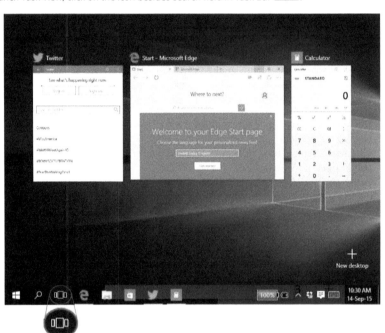.

Working with Virtual Desktops

From the Task View you can create and manage multiple desktops. Let's investigate virtual desktops more closely.

Creating Virtual Desktop

To create a virtual desktop follow these steps:

1- Open the Task View by clicking on the Task View button on the Task Bar.
2- On the bottom right, identify **New Desktop** button with a big plus sign. Click New Desktop. This instantly opens a new blank desktop called **Desktop 2**. If you point to Desktop 2 in Task View you will see a blank desktop with no open apps.

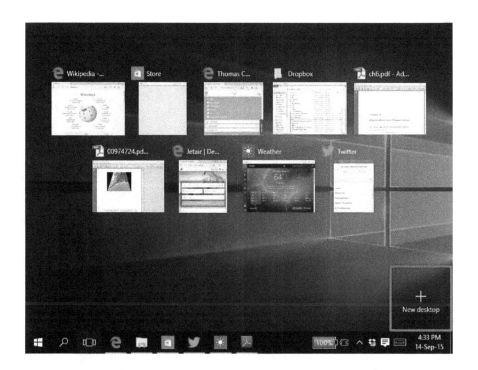

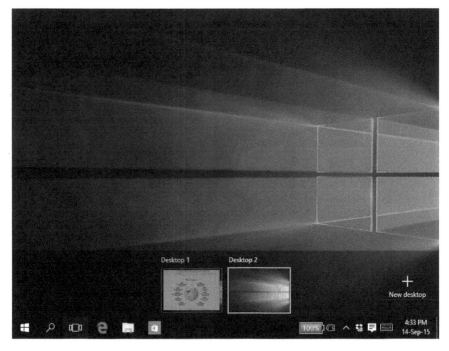

3- Task View also provides a preview of all the open desktops. You can scroll through all the open desktops using the arrow handles provided on each side.

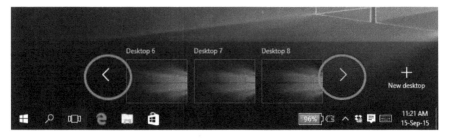

You may launch apps in the new desktop or you may sort running applications to different desktops. To illustrate sorting applications to various desktops, I have opened a number of apps; two Edge Browser windows and the weather app for vacation planning, two documents and one Edge Browser window for work. Click on the Task View button to get a preview of all the running apps. I intend to sort apps in two virtual desktops; one desktop for the project and other for vacation planning.

To sort apps to respective virtual desktops:

1- From the Task View, create a new virtual desktop **Desktop 2**.
2- Point to the first virtual desktop, the Task View shows thumbnails of all the open apps. Under the apps preview you can also see a thumbnail preview of all the open desktops. For now, you will see two thumbnails for Desktop 1 and Desktop 2.

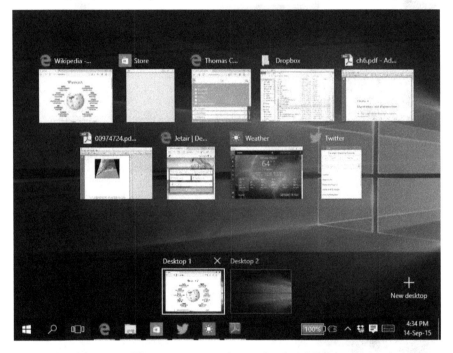

3- Select the preview of the app you want to place on the second desktop and drop it over the Desktop 2 preview. I am moving a pdf document to Desktop 2 for this example. As I click to select and drop app preview on desktop2, the thumbnail corresponding to the pdf document will be removed from Desktop 1 and instead shows up in Desktop 2. You can view all the apps running in desktop 2, by pointing to its thumbnail in Task View.

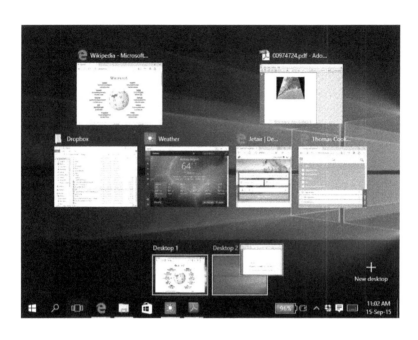

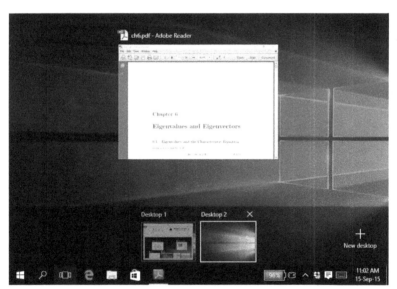

Alternatively;

1- Right click on the app preview in Task View that you wish to move to another desktop.
2- Select **Move To > Select Desktop**

Switch between virtual Desktops

You can easily switch between different desktops by:

1- Task View: Launch Task View and click on desktop thumbnail top open it. You can also use handles to navigate between desktops.
2- The second and handier way is with the keyboard shortcut **Windows Key + Ctrl + Left Arrow** and **Windows Key + Ctrl + Right Arrow.** With these keys you can cycle through virtual desktops.

Unfortunately, there is no way to quickly jump to a certain desktop. For example if I have 5 virtual desktops, I have to cycle through all desktops to move from desktop 1 to desktop 5; I cannot access desktop 5 directly.

Close a Desktop

To close a desktop simply point to the top-right corner of desktop thumbnail in Task View. This reveals a small red cross. Click the **x** button to close the desktop. All the apps opened in the desktop just closed are reverted to the previous desktop.

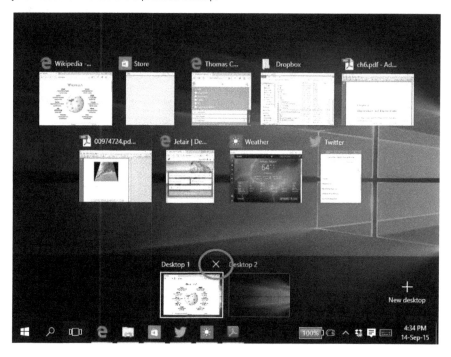

Pinning and Unpinning apps

As you continue to use your PC, you will be able to identify apps which you find more suited for your work than others. You might want to quickly access those applications on a regular basis. If so, you can easily pin those apps, either to your Task Bar or to the Start Menu.

To pin an app to the Start Menu/Task Bar:

1- Open the Start Menu and find the application you wish to pin.
2- Right-click on the app title. A pop-up menu appears with two options; **Pin to Start** and **Pin to Task Bar**
3- When you click on **Pin to Task Bar**, the icon from the app instantly appears on the Task Bar.
4- When you click on **Pin to Start**, the icon from the app instantly appears as tile in the right panel of the Start Menu. We will discuss the customization of Tiles in chapter 5.

To unpin an app from the Task Bar or Start Menu

1- Right-click on app which you wish to unpin.
2- Click **Unpin this program from Task Bar** or **Unpin from Start** as required. The app will be removed from the target.

Adding shortcuts to the Desktop

Alternative to pinning you can also add shortcuts of your apps to the desktop so you may be able to access them more quickly and easily. To create shortcuts of an application on your desktop, follow these steps:

1- Find the application for which you want to create a shortcut for from the Start Menu.
2- Click and drag the app icon out of the Start Menu and drop it on the desktop. You will see a small **Link** sign appearing with the icon you drag. Let go the icon. A shortcut has been created! The app will not be removed from the Start Menu. In the same way you may create shortcuts to files, folders etc. It is merely a copy of the shortcut which can be used to launch the app.

Enter& Exit Tablet Mode

Windows 10, like Windows 8 runs on both tablet and desktop computers and you can also effectively use the operating system on touch-enabled devices. When on a touch device, Windows 10 will adjust its interface to show the start screen which is similar to the right-panel of the Start Menu.

If you are working with hybrid devices such as Microsoft's Surface tablet, Windows 10 will detect when you detach the keyboard and will automatically switch you to Tablet Mode (after you confirm a prompt). You can also manually switch to Tablet Mode following these steps:

1- Open the Action Center from the Task Bar.

2- In the Quick Access settings identify the **Tablet Mode** button. (Note: If you cannot see the Tablet Mode button in the four buttons visible, click Expand to view all the quick settings buttons).

3- To go back to Desktop Mode, reopen the Action Center. If you are using a touch screen you can swipe from right corner of the screen to bring the Action Center. Tap/Click on the Tablet Mode button once again.

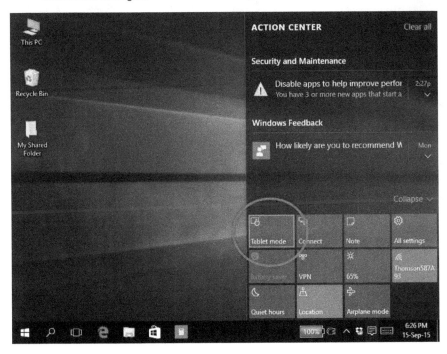

Locking your PC

If you intend to discontinue your work and move away from computer but do not want to turn it off completely, you may lock it. Once locked no one will be able to see your activity on your computer or access it. You can unlock the computer when you return to work by typing your User Account password or PIN.

To lock your computer follow these steps:

1- Click on Start button to open the **Start Menu**.
2- On the left-pane identify your User Account on the very top.
3- Right Click on your User Account. Select **Lock** from the context menu.

Sleep, Login, Restart & Shutdown

When you want to discontinue your work, you have the following options:

1- **Shut down computer**: If you opt to shut down your computer, all the applications you are running will be closed. The computer will turn off and will not use any electricity. You will need to reboot your computer and login with your PIN or password to your account.

2- **Sleep**: If you opt to put your computer to sleep, then the screen of your computer will be turned off and the computer will now enter a dormant state. Unlike when the computer is shut down, none of the applications are quit; they are temporarily halted (technically put into memory). You can resume your work from where you left fairly quickly. When in sleep mode the computer consumes less power. Many users prefer to put their computer to sleep rather than shutting it down.

3- **Restart**: The Restart option shuts down your computer and immediately turns it on again. Restart is necessary after installing or uninstalling apps, installing upgrades or fixing minor issues on your PC.

To sleep/Restart or Shut down your computer, open the Start Menu & click on **Power.** You will see a pop-up menu with options **Sleep Restart** or **Shut down**. Select one as required.

If you are using a laptop computer, then closing the lid automatically puts the computer to sleep, according to the default settings.

SECTION
3 PERSONALIZATION | Make it yours

Chapter 05

ESSENTIAL CUSTOMIZATION

Perhaps the first thing you will want to do with your PC as you get hang of it, is to personalize it. This chapter discusses some essential customization settings for Windows 10.

Customizing Desktop

There are a number of desktop settings available to you within the Windows 10 OS. Let's investigate each in detail.

Desktop Background& Color

Certainly the image you will see most often on your PC is your Desktop background, also called wallpaper. To change the wallpaper follow these steps:

1- Right-click on the desktop
2- Select Personalize from the context menu.

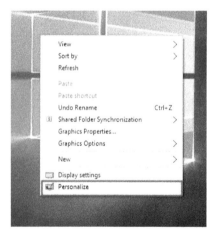

Alternatively

1- Open the Start Menu.
2- Click on **Settings**.
3- Go to **Personalize**. The window opens Background from the left-menu.

When selecting a background for your desktop, you have the following options in the **Background** drop-down box:

1- **Picture:** Select a picture from preset pictures provided in Windows. Click on the small image preview to change the wallpaper. Click on the **Browse** button to browse for a picture from your gallery and set it as wallpaper.
2- **Solid color:** Select a solid color for your background.
3- **Slideshow:** Display a slideshow of your pictures from a selected picture folder. The desktop background rotates pictures from your selected directory pausing on each picture for a few seconds before proceeding to the next.

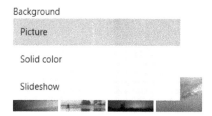

When you choose the Slideshow option, Windows will ask you the folder from which you want to display pictures. Click on browse to navigate and choose the desired folder for the slideshow. By default, images from the **Pictures** folder are shown as wallpapers.

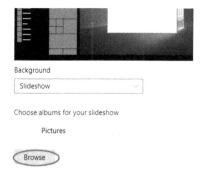

All settings will be applied in real time and you can click the cross button to exit the personalization menu at anytime.

Like the background, you may also select the color scheme for your desktop. Open the Color Menu from the left-hand menu. Choose a color from the preset options.

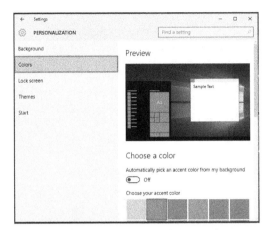

Screen Resolution

Screen resolution, in simple terms, means the amount of detail (technically pixels) to show on your computer screen (along with the width and height). The higher the resolution, the greater the detail, and the smaller the objects appearing on the screen. You may want to change the screen resolution to make objects appear larger, showing clearer screen details, or vice versa by the following steps:

1- From the Start Menu go to **Settings**
2- Open the **System** icon in the Settings window.
3- Select **Display** from the left-hand side menu to reveal more display related settings.
4- Scroll down to the bottom and click **Advanced Settings**.
5- Select the required screen resolution from the dropdown menu and hit the **Apply** button. The new resolution will be applied instantly and you will be prompted, asking you if you want to keep the new settings. You will also find a counter on the prompt window, which counts down from 15. The new resolution will be applied if within the duration of counter you fail to click "**Keep changes**". You may need to sign in again for the new resolution to take effect.

What is the countdown for?

From the list of available screen resolutions you may select a screen resolution that your computer screen is incapable of rendering. In such a case the screen may black out or may appear twisted. If this happens, computer reverts the settings back as the counter hits zero (i.e. after 15 seconds) so that you are not stuck with a blank/twisted screen without access to the visualizations to make additional changes.

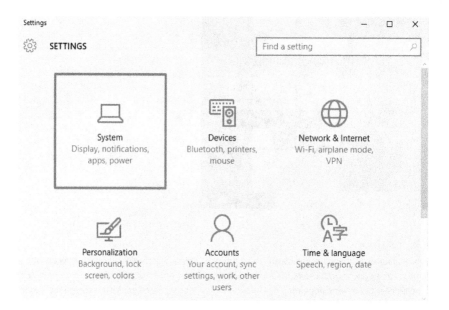

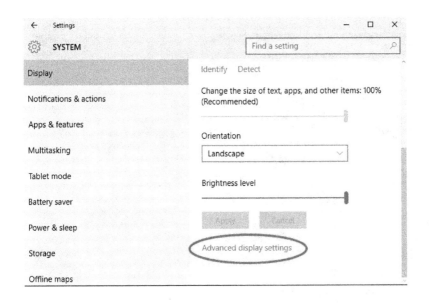

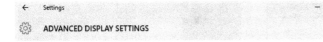

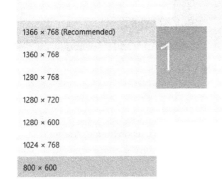

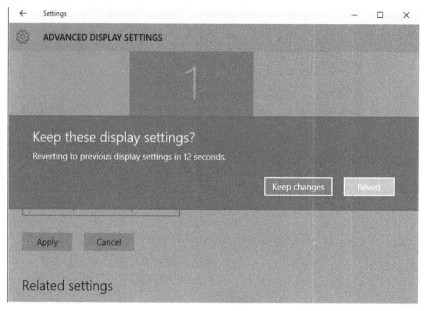

At 800 x 600

At 1280 x 768

When you leave your system unattended for a while, your system will log you out and lock the screen to prevent unauthorized use. You can set the image graphic set on the lock screen by following these steps:

1- From the Start Menu go to **Settings**
2- Open the **Personalization** icon in the Settings window.

3- Select **Lock Screen** from the left-hand side menu to reveal more display related settings.
   a. Select from the Dropdown box under Background:
   b. **Windows Spotlight:** Similar to Bing's image of the day. For every image you see on your lock screen you can provide feedback; if it is to your liking or not. If not, Windows will fetch a different style for you.
   c. **Background:** Choose from images preset in Windows 10
   d. **Slideshow:** Select an image folder on your PC to display a slideshow of your very own pictures.
4- You may also select apps to give a detailed status on your locked screen such as the Weather app or the Calendar app.

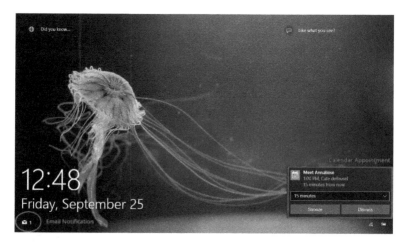

Customizing Action Center

By now we have already seen the Action Center. The Action Center can tremendously boost your productivity if customized appropriately. Thankfully Windows lets you customize almost every aspect of Action Center; from controlling the notifications to the background color of the panel are customizable. Let's explore in detail.

Customizing Quick Actions

1- From the Start Menu go to **Settings**
2- Open the **System** icon in Settings window.
3- Select **Notification & Action** from the left-hand side menu to reveal more settings.
4- You will find various settings for *Quick Actions* and *Notifications*.
5- When collapsed the Action Center shows only 4 system icons. By default, the Action Center shows the shortcuts to Tablet Mode, Connect, Note, All Settings. You can customize the icons and choose which 4 icons appear. To change the icons, identify four tiles under Quick Actions. Click on an individual icon and select the desired shortcut from the list. For this example I am changing in Tablet Mode, the Wi-Fi settings.

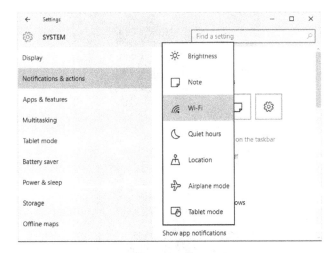

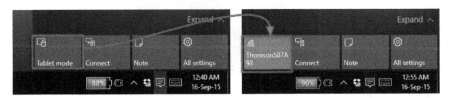

To customize notifications

6- From the Start Menu go to **Settings**

7- Open the **System** icon in the Settings window.

8- Select **Notification & Action** from the left-hand side menu.

9- You will find various settings for *Quick Actions* and *Notifications*.

10- Scroll down to **Notifications**. Under notifications you will find a list of apps which are allowed to notify you via the Action Center. From here you can turn off notifications from any app by toggling the switch off. Alternatively, if you wish to avoid notifications from a particular app, simply right-click on the last notification generated by the app and click **Turn off notifications for this app** from the context menu.

You can customize the display of Action Center by changing its color and transparency. You can change the theme color of the Action Center from the **Color** menu in **Personalization**, as detailed in the Background & Color section in this chapter.

Showing colors in the Action Center

To change the color of the entire Action Center panel follow these steps:

1- Open the Start Menu.
2- Click on **Settings**.
3- Go to **Personalize**.
4- Open **Colors** menu.
5- Scroll down and identify the option "Show colors on Start, Task Bar and Action Center". Toggle the switch as required.
6- Select color from the above palette.

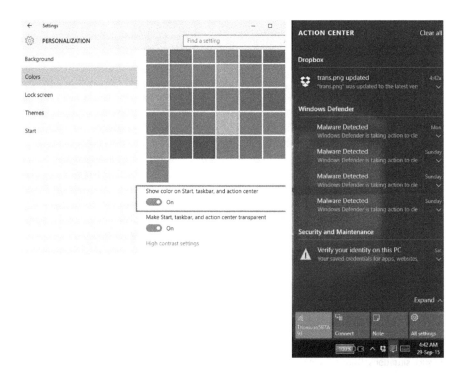

Changing Transparency

To change the transparency follows these steps:

7- Open the Start Menu.
8- Click on **Settings**.
9- Go to **Personalize**.
10- Open **Colors** menu.
11- Scroll down and identify the option "Make Start, Task Bar and Action Center transparent". Toggle the switch as required.

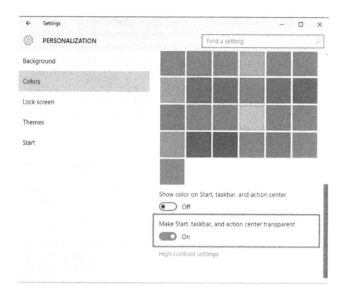

Quiet Hours

Often there are times when notifications can hinder your work flow. Quiet Hours can be your friend in such situations. During Quiet Hours you are not notified via the Action Center. To turn on quiet hours:

1- In the Task Bar identify the **Notification icon** for the Action Center
2- Right click to reveal a context menu.
3- Click **Turn on Quiet Hours**

When using Windows 10 on your tablet you can also set one of the quick actions to Quiet hours. In setting, you simply tap Quiet hours in the Action Center to dismiss upcoming notifications.

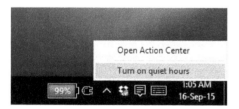

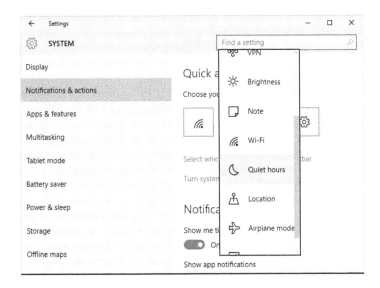

Customizing Start Menu

We have already explored the Start Menu in previous chapters and have also discussed a few options for Start Menu customization such as color, transparency etc. In this section we will explore options for customizing the **Start Menu**.

Customizing the Left Pane

You can customize the left panel of the Start Menu to show the most used apps and/or recently added apps. However, you cannot allow the Start Menu to show a custom app lists. You can, however, remove a certain app from showing up in the list.

To hide/show list of most used apps:

1- From the Start Menu open the **Settings** app
2- Click on **Personalization**.
3- Select Start from left-menu.
4- Toggle the switch for **Most used apps** on/off.

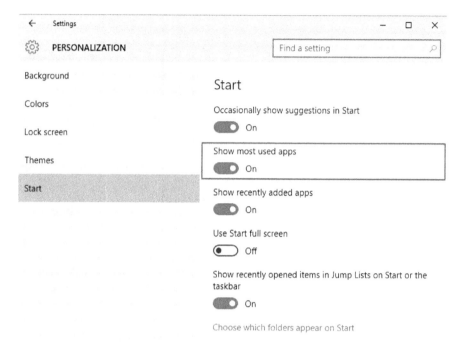

To hide specific items from the list of most used apps, follow these steps:

1- Identify the icon of the app you want to remove from the list.
2- Right-click the icon
3- Click **Don't show in this list**

The app can still be accessed from the **all apps** option in the Start Menu, nevertheless, now it will not show up in the left panel. While the left panel presents fewer customization options, the right panel, comprised of tiles is quiet flexible. For every tile you can do the following actions:

Pinning & Moving Tiles

We have already seen how you can pin apps to the Start Menu. Another simpler way to pin apps to the Start Menu is by simply dragging and dropping apps onto the right-hand side panel of your Start Menu. The app will appear as a tile. You can move the tile above or below the existing tiles by grabbing and dragging the tile up/down.

Creating & Naming Groups of Tiles

You can drag & drop apps on the Start Menu and create groups of related apps. You can also click to edit the group title. To add a title to a group, hover your mouse over the right-side of the app group to show the menu button. Click the menu button to make the title editable. Add your title.

To edit the title of an existing group, simply click on the title to make it editable.

Unpin Tiles

You may want to get rid of some of the pre-installed tiles. To remove apps tiles, simply right-click on the tiles and click **Unpin from Start Menu**, the app tile will be removed.

  To reveal the context menu for the tiles on a touch device, long tap the tile.

Resizing Tiles

Naturally, you may prefer larger tiles for frequently accessed apps to make them easily distinguishable. You can resize the tile size by following these steps:

1- Right-click (or long tap) the tile.
2- Select resize-> Select size

Different sizes are available for different apps. For example, you can resize the Map tile to small, medium, wide large; while for OneNote you can only select small, medium or wide sizes.

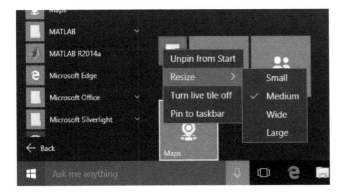

Turning Live On/Off

Live Tiles are able to update themselves over the internet to bring in fresh content to you. You can turn off/on the Live feature of a tile to restrict them from updating.

Turning off the Live Tile feature to make a Live Tile static, follow these steps:

1- Right-click (or long tap) the tile.
2- Turn Live Tile off

Why turn Live Tile off?
Live Tiles update over internet and consume internet bandwidth. The Live feature can become less desirable when you are using mobile data or your internet bandwidth is limited.

Switch to Start Screen

Users who wish to use Windows 10 on tablets, can choose between a regular desktop or a start screen when they start their system. In the case of selecting a start screen as the startup option, the Start Menu will be your primary interface replacing the desktop; the desktop will only be accessible via File Explorer. To select the Start screen as your launch option, follow these steps:

5- From the Start Menu open the **Settings** app
6- Click on **Personalization**.
7- Select Star from left-menu.
8- Toggle the switch for **Use Start full Screen** on.

Customizing Task Bar

Auto-Hide Task Bar

You may auto-hide the Task Bar. If set, you can access the Task Bar only when you point your mouse to the Task Bar location.

1- Right-click on the Task Bar.
2- Click **Properties**
3- In the **Task Bar** tab, check box beside the **Auto-Hide the Task Bar**

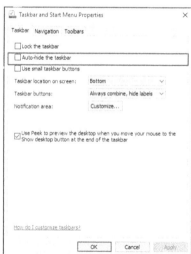

You can also control the icons to be displayed in the right most corner of the Task Bar, also called the system tray by:

1- From the Start Menu go to **Settings**
2- Open the **System** icon in the Settings window.
3- Select **Notification & Action.**
4- Click on select **which icons appear on the Task Bar.** This will populate a list of programs with toggle switches. Turn the visibility on/off for each program as desired.

Automatic Sleep Time

In the last chapter we learned that using **Sleep** mode is often considered a better alternative to **Shutting Down**. When the computer is put to sleep it consumes less energy and takes less time to resume. You may also choose to put the computer into sleep mode in case you leave the computer unattended for a certain period of time. Setting up sleep times can maximize battery life (for your laptop) and help conserve energy. To set up an automatic sleep timer for your computer, follow these steps:

1- From the Start Menu go to **Settings**
2- Open the **System** icon in the Settings window.
3- Select **Power & Sleep** from the left-hand side menu to reveal more display related settings.
4- The window provides two settings; when to turn the display/screen off and when to turn the PC to sleep under **Screen** and **Sleep** respectively. For each setting you can specify behaviors; when your laptop is using battery power, or when it is plugged in a power source. Select time intervals as required from the dropdown boxes. As a general rule, you will want to keep the time interval shorter when the laptop is using battery power to conserve energy for a longer period.

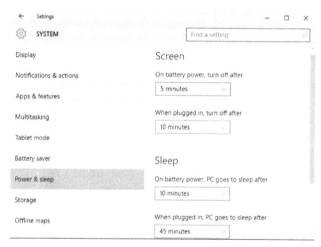

SECTION
4
FILE MANAGEMENT & SEARCH

Chapter 06

UNDERSTANDING FILES, FOLDERS &DRIVES

Perhaps your computers wouldn't be of much use if you weren't able to store your files on it. Long gone are the days when computers were only good for saving files on a hard disk and users had to rely on floppy disks for additional space. Modern computers are powerful enough to store hundreds of thousands of file types, like music, videos, documents and other files. With the ease of storing such large amounts of data comes the challenge of managing files. Thankfully, Window's filing system is designed to facilitate users who are struggling to manage enormous amounts of data on their PC.

This chapter introduces you to the Windows Filing system. Basic knowledge of Windows Filing is essential for efficient file management. We will also talk about basic filing terminology. If you are comfortable with terms such as files, disks and folders, feel free to skip to next chapter.

Various Elements of Windows Filing System

Windows Filing System is analogous to the traditional real-world filing cabinet. Just like you organize files in manila folders and store them in your filing cabinet; in the same way you save files in folders on your hard drive.

What is a file?

A file is actually a simple item which is used to store information. Information stored in a file may be of any type; it may be an image, a typed document, a spreadsheet, a video or an audio file. A file on a computer is represented by:

1- A *File Name*
2- *Icon*: The associated icon to the file makes the file type itself easy to decipher. Icons are specific to file types. As you continue to use your PC, you will identify icons for commonly used types of files.
3- *File Extension*: File extensions, like icons, are specific to the type of file. File extensions are usually hidden by default.

File Icon

CTC_Spain_ (CTC_Spain_Plan)File Name
plan.pdf (.pdf) File Extension

You may not realize that you've worked with files daily on your computer in the past. If you are reading a digital book, chances are that you are actually reading a pdf file. Likewise, if you are listening to music or viewing photos in an image library, you are using an audio file, or an image file respectively. You can send/receive files as attachments in emails as well.

Consider that you use an internet browser to visit a webpage. Information on a webpage is stored on a remote server and therefore you are not interacting with a file on a local disk. However if you wish to save the webpage to your computer, then you may treat the (offline) webpage as a file (on your hard disk).

What is a folder?

As you start working with your PC, you will find yourself creating files very often. Searching for a desired file in an unorganized accumulation of files can be time an energy consuming. Folders come in handy here. Folders are containers for your files. You can organize files in folders much like you would do with physical files in manila folders in a filing cabinet.

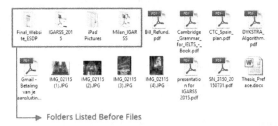

Folders Listed Before Files

Folders can contain other folders and files. Folders contained within other folders are called **sub-folders**. Note how the icons for folders look like manila folders.

Where are the files stored?

All the files, folders (even the operating system i.e. Windows 10 and programs) are stored on the hard disk of your computer. Hard disks are physical disks sealed inside your PC's case. You can consider disks to be your computer's filing cabinets. You can store and access files to and from the hard disk using your file managing software i.e. Windows File Explorer. The primary hard drive on which the operating system is installed is historically denoted by **C:**

 Hard drive or hard disk or fixed disks are interchangeable terms

What are Libraries?

Organizing files in folders on your PC is a tedious task. Windows provides libraries to help you quickly organize files according to their type. There are four default libraries:

1- **Document Library:** Use the document library to store spreadsheets, word-processing documents, notes, presentations etc.
2- **Music Library:** Use the Music Library to store audio files and organize music.
3- **Picture Library:** Use the Image Library to store image files and organize music.
4- **Video Library:** Use the Video Library to store video files and organize Video.

Files saved/copy/moved in Document, Music, Picture and Video libraries are stored in My Documents, My Music, My Pictures and My Videos, respectively.

You can think of your Library as a super folder. With Libraries you can show the content of several folders (instead of content from a single folder). By default Documents/Music/Images and Videos Libraries only shows files contained in their respective folders within that Library. However, you can configure each library to include and show files from other folders as well.

By default, Libraries are not shown in Windows 10 File Explorer. We will review steps to enable Libraries when we revisit File Explorer in chapter 9.

Windows Folder Structure

Windows already provides sub-folders such as Pictures, Music, Downloads, and Documents etc. where you can store relevant files. All these (sub) folders are contained inside a folder associated to your User Account. Shortcuts of these folders appear in *My PC* and in File Explorer to facilitate quick access. Also **File history** – a tool in Windows 10 to backup your files- includes all these folders for backup by default. Therefore, it is recommended that you store files inside the folders provided. As we proceed in this section, all of these concepts will become more easily understood.

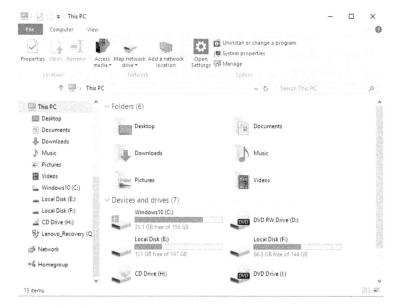

If your PC is used by different family member(s)/or individual(s), you can make use of User Accounts in Windows. With User Accounts, users can keep their files and system preferences separate. If you set up User Accounts for different people, every user will be allocated a folder (inside the **Users** folder in the main Windows folder on drive C:) where they can store their files. Other users on the system will not have access to these files.

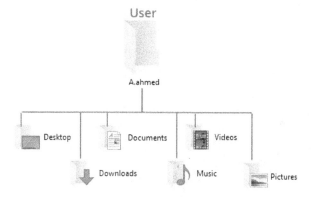

Chapter 07
USING THE FILE EXPLORER

The File Explorer (formerly known as Windows Explorer) is the tool in which you will use to manage files, folders and libraries on your disk drive. File Explorer facilitates users to access and manage files by providing additional tools such as searching, sorting, copying and deleting files, etc. The File Explorer has been an integral part of the Windows Operating System since it was first introduced to the world in Microsoft's debut OS, Windows 95. In the next few chapters, we will learn about File Explorer, and how you can use it to effectively manage files on your disk drive.

Launching File Explorer

To open File Explorer:

1- Click on Start button to open the Start Menu
2- Identify and click on the **File Explorer** button

Alternatively

1- Click on the **File Explorer** button on the Task Bar

 From the keyboard, use short cut **Windows Key + E** to launch File Explorer.

File Explorer Interface

The File Explorer can display files and folders in a varied layout. At the very least, the interface has the following basic sections:

1- **Navigation Panel:** Navigation Panel spans the vertical column on the left side of the window. The panel enlists various destinations on your computer; My PC, Desktop, Documents etc. You can expand to show subfolders inside of a particular folder by clicking on the small arrow beside the folder icon. The Navigation panel in Windows 10 features a **Quick Access** panel towards the top.

2- **Main Window/Folder:** The main window which lies to the right-hand side of the navigation panel, details the contents of the folder you have selected from the navigation panel.

3- **Path:** Path shows your current location when navigating within the filing system. For example, in figure below, you can view the content of folder *Season 2*; the path gives my complete address i.e. *This PC -> Downloads -> Curious George -> Season 2*. I can go one (or more) step(s) up in the folder's hierarchy by clicking on any of the folders listed in the path. Clicking on Curious George Folder from the path will take you one step up and display the contents of the Curious George folder.

4- **Back Button:** The Back button takes you to the last viewed destination/folder.

Do not worry if you see a few more panels/menus in your File Explorer, we will revisit File Explorer layout to investigate other panels in detail.

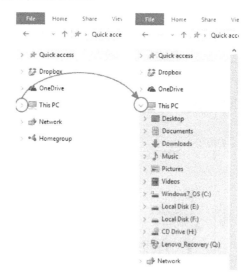

Ribbon Menu

Windows 10 introduces the typical ribbon menu to the File Explorer which is common in most applications built by Microsoft, such as the office Suite. In this section, we will investigate the ribbon menu for File Explorer in detail.

Click on **File, Home, Share** or **View** tab to show the ribbon menu; click anywhere from within File Explorer to hide the ribbon.

- **File Menu:** From the File menu you can open a new File Explorer window, access frequently used documents under "Frequent Places".
- **Home Menu**: The Home Menu gives you shortcuts to common folder tasks such as create, copy, move, rename etc. We will learn about every task in chapter 8.
- **Share Menu**: You can share documents directly from the File Explorer from the Share menu. Sharing files via the share menu will be discussed later in this chapter.
- **View Menu**: The View menu provides you with options to change the layout and view of the folder panel. We will discuss View panel in detail in chapter 9 when we discuss managing files using File Explorer.

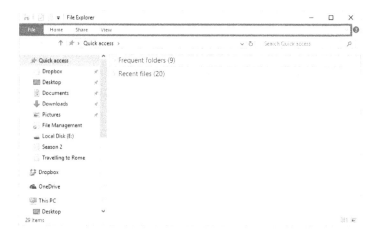

Pinning Ribbon Menu

By default the ribbon menu hides as soon as you click anywhere within a folder. If you find ribbons in File Explorer handy, you can pin them. The Pinned ribbon menu becomes permanently available to you i.e. the ribbon will not disappear on clicking away from the menu.

To use the pin ribbon menu in File Explorer follow these steps:

1- Open the Ribbon menu by clicking on any of the tabs (home, view , share)
2- Identify and click on the small pin button besides the question-mark.

You can also use the up/down button to show/hide the ribbon menu.

Using the File Explorer to Navigate

By now we know our files are stored on the computers physical hard drive, which resides inside the PC's case, and File Explorer acts like a bridge between the user and the disk, giving the user access to the files. We have also briefly talked about Windows file structure. In this section, we will use File Explorer to navigate through the hard disk to better understand the Windows Filing structure.

 My Computer is now **MY PC** in Windows 10

Where is my data?

Generally, you will use Documents, Pictures, Videos, the Music folder and occasionally, the Desktop folder to save your files to. All the files you download from the internet will be saved to the Downloads folder. All these folders are saved on your **C** drive, somewhere inside the Windows folders. Let's demonstrate this with a simple example:

1- Launch File Explorer, click on **This PC**. This PC is just like your gateway to your computer's file cabinet.
2- You will see that the folder panel displays two sections; **Folders**(6) and Devices and **Drives**(7) for my system. Note that the count of items may differ on your PC.
3- You will find frequently used folders such as Pictures, Documents under the **Folders** section. By looking at the structure of **This PC** you may think that the folders are stored in **The PC** folder; however, this is not the case. The user folders are located inside the drive, listed in the Device section. To check the location of the folder on the disk, right-click on the folder. For this example I will right-click on the **Desktop** folder. Then I will select **Properties** from the context menu.
4- A pop-up window titled **Desktop properties** will appear. Go to the **Location** tab and find the *real* location of the folder from the path provided. From the screenshot below you will see that the Desktop folder is actually located on the **C** drive. If we want to access the folder on the **C** Drive, we will have to follow the path i.e. From **C Drive** *(go to)* user folder *(go to)* A.ahmed *(go to)* Desktop. Most definitely your path will look the same except for the "A.ahmed". This folder derives its name from the username of account which I use to login to the computer.

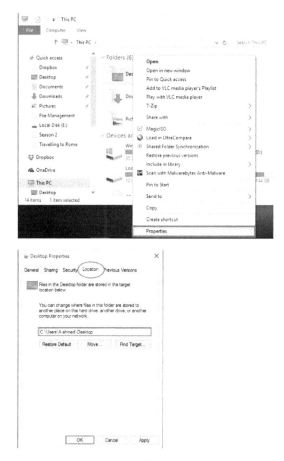

Navigating the Windows Filing Structure

1- Having seen that the folders are buried somewhere inside the **C** Drive, now let's go to the actual location. Note that you can also go to the actual location by clicking on the **Find Target** button in the pop-up window. However, I recommend using File Explorer to navigate to the location on the **C Drive,** to get better understanding of Windows file organization.

2- From **My PC**, open **C Drive**. Your Drive may have a name. The **C** Drive on my computer is named **Widnows10**. Do not confuse Drive name with drive letter. Drive letter are always enclosed in brackets. Drive **C** stores your operating system and all your programs.

3- You will see a number of folders on the **C Drive** (depending upon your system and programs). Do not be intimidated by all the folders. You will never interact with most of the folders here! Here is a summary of what is going on:

    a. **Windows:** Folders named as Windows, contain files related to your operating system. If you have upgraded from Windows 7/8, then most certainly you will see a folder named 'Windows.old'.

    b. **Program Files & Program Files (x86)**: These folders contain your apps. For each app there is a folder with app related files and the app itself. What you see in the **Start Menu** are app shortcuts.

    c. **User(s):** All of the user related data is saved in this folder. If you have multiple users, here you will find folder for every user.

4- Click on the folder corresponding to your User Account. In this folder you will find all of the folders for which you will use to save your data in, such as Videos, Music, Documents etc.

5- You have made it! You can now locate the destinations that files actually reside on your disk!

On a day-to-day basis, you will never to access the folders from the drive. Windows Explorer provides shortcuts to these destinations for quick access. However, it's good to know the location of files on the drive for troubleshooting purposes.

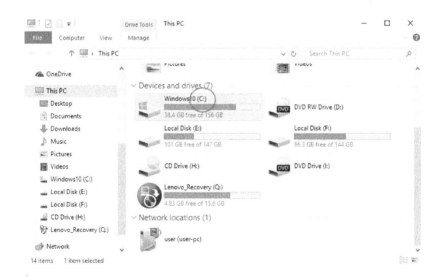

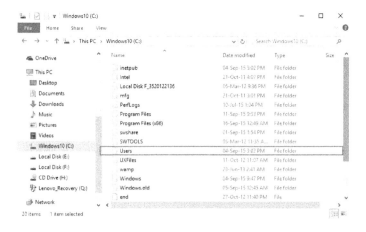

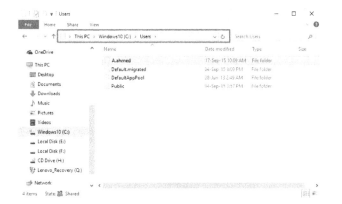

 Swshare/SWTools: If you have an IBM/Lenoveo system these folders contain files for performing a backup.

Quick Access

File Explorer opens a destination called "**Quick Access**" when you launch it; in other words, Quick Access is the File Explorer's start-up folder. Quick access, a new feature introduced in Windows 10, displays your most frequently viewed folders and most recently accessed individual files. Quick Access gives you a good jump start if you want to resume your work quickly.

 If you are upgrading from Windows 8/7 you will instantly note that Windows 10 introduces a new starting point when you launch File Explorer. Earlier, when you launched File Explorer, by default you were taken to **My computer** or **Favorites**. In contrast to **Favorites**, Quick Access also displays recent files (not only folders). The Quick Access feature combines **Recent Places** and **Favorites** from earlier versions of Windows.

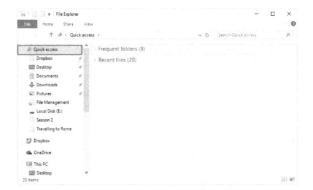

Pinning/Unpinning folders to Quick Access

You can pin folders to Quick Access so you may be able to reach them more quickly. To pin a folder to Quick Access:

1- In the Navigation Pane identify/navigate to the folder you wish to pin.
2- Right-click on the folder.
3- Click **Pin to Quick Access**

All the folders pinned to Quick Access have a small pin icon beside them.

Likewise you can unpin folders from Quick Access. To unpin a folder from Quick Access:

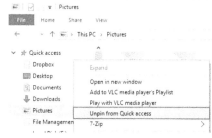

1- In the Navigation Pane identify the folder you wish to unpin from Quick Access.
2- Right-click on the folder.
3- Click **Unpin from Quick Access**

Sharing Files from File Explorer

Windows 10 enables you to share files quickly and easily directly from the File Explorer. You can select a folder, zip it directly from the share tab and send it via email. Or you can share your files using any of the apps which support the sharing feature to share the file. To share a picture via a social media app like Facebook, follow these steps:

1- Click on the image you want to share.
2- Click on the **Share** tab.
3- Click the **Share** icon in the Send Menu.
4- Choose the app which you will use to share. I am choosing the Facebook app for demonstration purposes.
5- Add status message and share!

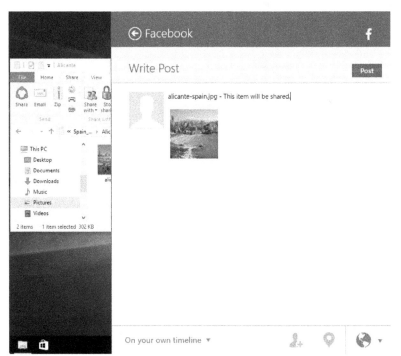

Introducing OneDrive

OneDrive is free online cloud storage which comes free of cost with every Microsoft account. Windows 10 heavily supports cloud storage with OneDrive, integrated into the operating system.

What is OneDrive?

You can think of OneDrive as a regular folder to store files; but here, the folder is not saved on your desktop or PC, it is actually saved on the Windows Servers over the internet. You can access this folder from anywhere; from your Windows Phone, Tablet, or on your PC, and even from an internet browser. Every Windows 10 powered device come with a OneDrive folder. Whenever you add file to this folder the file synchronizes with the OneDrive folder on the Windows Server and is made available on all the OneDrive folders across your devices. For example, you add a word document from your office PC to OneDrive. It will instantly synchronize and will be made available through OneDrive on all devices (on which you use the same Microsoft account). You can access and edit the document from the OneDrive folder on your home PC.

Even if you do not have Windows 10 powered tablet you can download and use OneDrive app for your tablet from iOS or Android stores.

Launching & Adding Files to OneDrive

You can launch OneDrive directly from the File Explorer. Alternatively you may also launch OneDrive from the Start Menu (from all apps list)

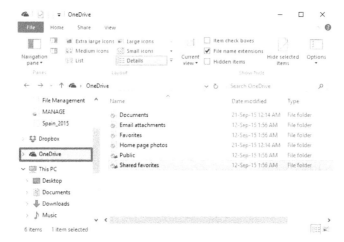

Since OneDrive is like a regular folder on your PC, you can add files and folders to OneDrive in the same way as you would transfer files and folders to any other folder on your PC. You can drag & drop files, copy and paste files, or save files to OneDrive directly from apps. We will discuss moving and copying files to folders in next chapter.

As pointed out earlier, when you add files to OneDrive, they are synchronized and made available on all the devices associated with your Microsoft account. A small icon appears with every file/folder in OneDrive indicating its synchronizing status.

Documents

The folder and its constituent files are synchronized over the internet. All the content of the folder is available across all the associated devices via OneDrive.

Spain_2015

The folder and its contents are synchronizing. The contents are not yet available on other devices. Once all the files are synchronized this icon changes to green-tick, indicating successful synchronization. Remember the time it takes to synchronize a file depends on its size as well as the strength of your internet connection. If you are in a location with no working internet connection, then your files will not be synchronized; however synchronization starts as soon as internet access becomes available. Unsynchronized files are still available to use on the local system.

Chapter 08
COMMON FILES& FOLDER OPERATIONS

In this chapter we will cover the basics of file management, starting from how to create folder and organize files in folders. We will move forward to common folder related tasks such as copying, moving, deleting etc. If you feel you are proficient with these operations, feel free to jump to the next chapter.

Create new Folder

You can create a folder in a number of different ways. Let's see them step-by-step.

Creating folder from the Home Menu in the File Explorer Ribbon

1- Open destination folder where you want to create a new folder.
2- Open the **Home** menu from the File Explorer ribbon
3- Click on the **New Folder** button
4- Name the folder as required. By default, it will be called "New Folder"

Creating Folder from Context Menu

1- Open destination folder where you want to create a new folder.
2- Right-click in the folder panel to show the context menu.
3- Go to **New-> Folder**
4- Name the folder as required. By default it will be called "New Folder"

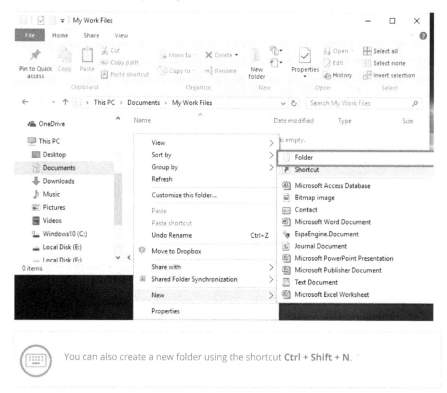

You can also create a new folder using the shortcut **Ctrl + Shift + N.**

Moving File/Folders with File Explorer

You can use File Explorer for managing and organizing your files and folders. To move a folder to another folder, follow these steps. For the purpose of demonstration I am moving **Wallpaper** folder from **Downloads** folder to **Pictures** folder.

1- Open the parent folder containing the folder for which you intend to move. The Wallpaper folder is located inside the *Downloads* folder, so I will open the *Downloads* folder.
2- Scroll to the folder you want to move. Click and drag the folder to the destination folder in the Navigation Panel. I will click to select *Wallpaper* folder and drag it on the *Picture* folder in

the navigation panel. You will see a small label **Move to <designation folder name>.** For this example, the label says, **Move to Pictures**

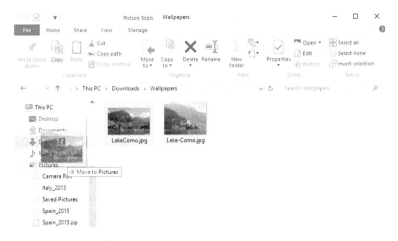

Moving multiple files/folders

You can select multiple files and folders and drag them to destination folder to move/sort files and folders in batches. You may drag and drop multiple files/folders to destination in the navigation pane in File Explorer, or you may drag and drop multiple folders/files on other folders in the folder panel of File Explorer to move them.

To select multiple folders click on the first folder, followed by clicking on the second folder while holding the CTRL key on your keyboard.

To select a row of continuous images click on the first image, SHIFT, click on the last image. All the images between the first and last image will be selected.

Let's see with an example. I have a few images from Spain, Barcelona and Alicante. Let's organize these image files in folders.

1. I have created two subfolders called **Alicante, Barcelona and Spain_2015** inside the folder **Pictures**.
2. **Selecting Images of Alicante:** To select images of Alicante, I will click on one the first image and hold the CTRL key down on the keyboard and click on the second image. This selects both the images.
3. **Move images of Alicante to *Alicante* folder:** While the images are selected, click on any of the two images and drag them onto the *Alicante* folder. This will move both the images to

Alicante folder. Note that a small [2] appears on the images to indicate that you are moving two files inside a folder.

4- Now to move four images of Barcelona to *Barcelona* folder I will click to select the first image of Barcelona, and hold the Shift key down on the keyboard and select the last image, selecting all four *continuous images.* Click on any one of the images and drag on to *Barcelona* folder to move all 4 images to *Barcelona* folder.

5- **Moving folders to other folders**: After sorting images to their respective folders. I will select both, *Barcelona* and *Alicante* folders (as in step 2), and drag them to the Spain_2015 folder in the Pictures folder. All done!

Note that for this example we moved multiple files and folders by dragging them onto folders in the folders pane of File Explorer, unlike the previous example where we moved folders by dragging and dropping them onto folders in the navigation pane of File Explorer.

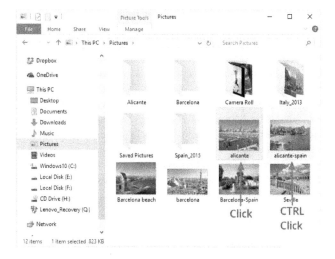

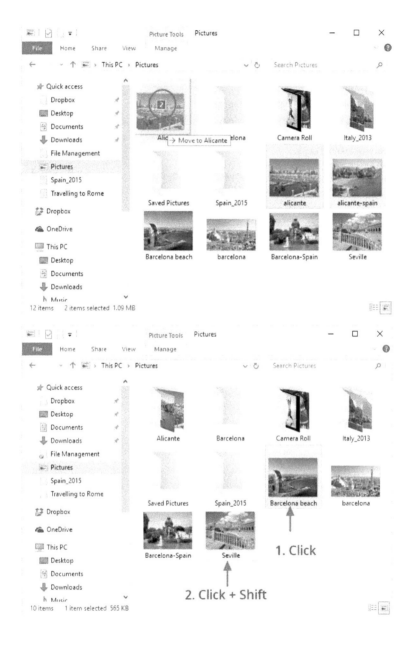

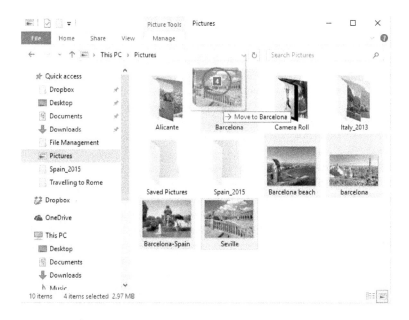

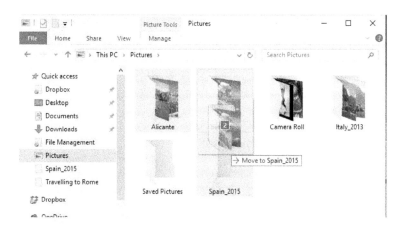

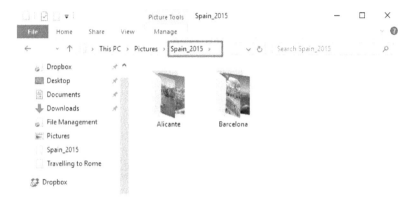

An alternative way to move a folder to another location:

1- Select the folder/file you want to move.
2- Open the **Home** menu from the ribbon.
3- Click on **Move to.** A list of recently used folders will appear. Click to Select a folder where you want to move. If the destination folder does not show up on the menu, click on **Choose Location** and select the destination folder.

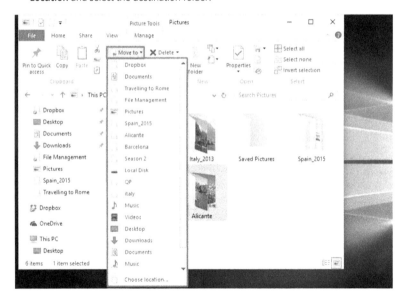

Copy Folders through File Explorer

Moving files from one folder to another, removes the files from the first location and transfers it to the second location. If you want to that the file appears in both the location, you should choose the **Copy** Action. To copy a file, follow these steps:

1- Select the folder/file you want to move.
2- Open the **Home** menu from the ribbon.
3- Click on **Copy to.** A list of recently used folders will appear. Click on the destination folder. If the destination folder does not show up on the list, click on **Choose Location** and select the destination folder.

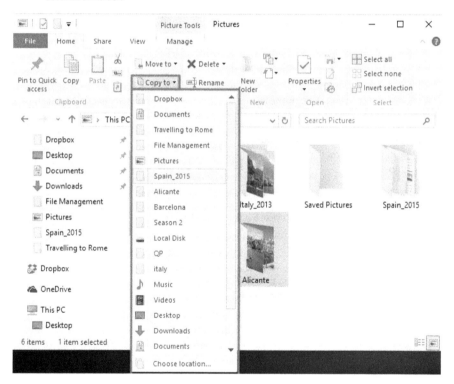

Tip Copy vs. Move when Dragging & Dropping

When you move a file/folder within a drive the default action is **Move**. When you move files/folders from an external drive to the local drive or vice versa, the default action is **Copy**.

You can also use the keyboard shortcut Ctrl + C to copy and Ctrl + P to paste the copy of file to the second location.

While moving file/folders press CTRL; this will copy the file/folders instead of moving them

Renaming Folder

It is a good habit to appropriately name folders so you'll be able to find them quickly. To rename a folder follow these steps:

1- Select the folder you want to rename.
2- Right-click to show the context menu.
3- Click **Rename.**

Alternatively

Click the folder you wish to rename twice, but with a small pause between the two clicks. The name of the folder becomes editable.

Alternatively

1- Select the folder/file you want to move.
2- Open the **Home** menu from the ribbon.
3- Click **Rename**

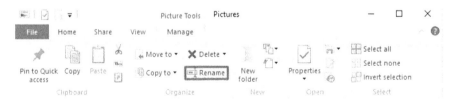

You can also use the keyboard shortcut **F2** to rename a folder.

Delete & Restore Files

Deleting extra files can help you keep clutter away from your PC. Following are a few common ways of deleting a file:

1- Click on the folder/file you wish to delete and press the **Del** button on the keyboard.
2- Click to select and then drag and drop file/folder to the **Recycle Bin** on the desktop to delete it.
3- Right-click on the file/folder you wish to delete and select **Delete** from the context menu.
4- Click to select the file/folder you wish to delete and choose **Delete** from the **Home** tab on the ribbon menu.

Every time you attempt to delete any item, a notification will appear to confirm your action. Click **Yes** to confirm. All the files which are deleted are moved to the Recycle Bin. You can restore files from the Recycle Bin at any time. Note that since files in the Recycle Bin are not completely removed they still occupy space on your disk. If you want to delete files to free space on your disk then choose to permanently delete files/folders, by emptying the Recycle Bin. Once the Recycle Bin is emptied, the files are gone forever.

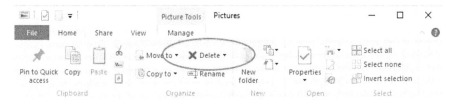

Permanently Delete Files/Folders

To permanently delete files follow one of the steps:

1- Click on the folder/file you wish to permanently delete and press the **Del** button on keyboard.
2- Empty Recycle Bin. All the items in the Recycle Bin will be permanently deleted.

 To Permanently Delete an item hold **SHIFT** and Press DEL key on your keyboard. The file will bypass Recycle Bin. Note that the confirmation prompt asks you if you want to *permanently delete* (as opposed to *delete*)

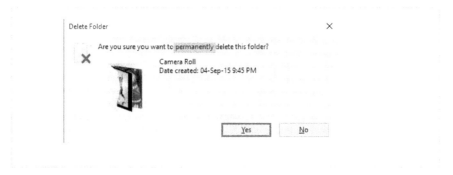

Restoring Files

Files which have not been permanently deleted can be restored from the Recycle Bin. To restore one or more files, open the Recycle Bin. Select the file you want to restore. Right click on the file and click **restore** from the context menu.

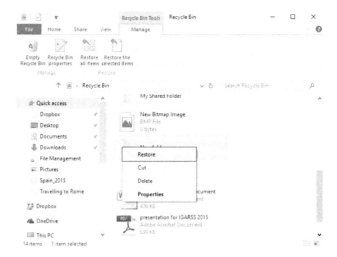

Zipping/Unzipping Folders

Think of a situation when you have to attach 50 files in an email. Since you cannot email a folder to anyone, uploading individual file will take lot of time and energy, right? Zipping (compressing) files is a practical solution to this problem. You can create a folder, add all your files, zip or compress the folder and attach the compressed folder as an attachment. The receiver will uncompress/extract the files from the zipped folder to access all of the files contained in the folder.

Let's see how you can compress and extract files on Windows 10.

1- To compress a folder right-click on the folder to show the context menu.
2- Point to Send to -> Compressed. Your folder will be zipped.

Unzipping Folder

If you receive a zipped file you can still view the content in zipped file however all the content is read-only. You may not be able to edit a word file within a zipped folder unless you extract it. To uncompress/unzip a zipped file and access the content of the folder follow these steps.

1- Select the zipped folder and click the **Compressed Folder Tools** tab, and then click **Extract all**.
2- Alternatively, you can also drag files you want to extract from the zipped folder to a new location.

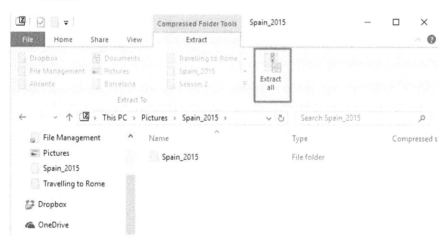

Besides using zip files for mailing multiple files, zip files offer other advantages too.

1- Zipped files consume less disk space. Old files can be zipped and archived.

2- As Zipped files take up much less space, emailing a zipped file also consumes less bandwidth.

 When extracting if you see the Extract all button is inactive then make sure you have opened the file in File Explorer. You can do this by:
1- Right-click on zipped file.
2- Open with-> File Explorer

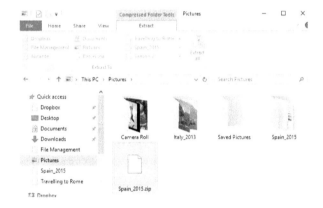

Pinning Folders to Start Menu

You can pin folders which you frequently access to the Start Menu.

1- Select the folder you want to pin
2- Right-click on the folder. Select **Pin to Start** from context menu.

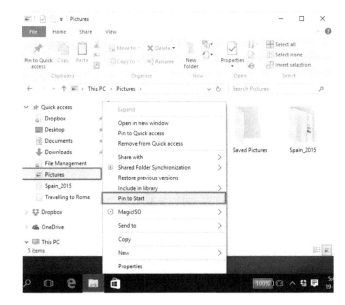

File explore offers a number of tools to organize your files and folders. In this chapter we will learn about the use of the File Explorer to organize and manage files and folders.

Customizing File Explorer

By default, when you open a folder in File Explorer, the folders are listed before the files. You can customize the arrangement of the File Explorer to facilitate your everyday task of file management and organization.

Changing View

The files and folders appear in **_Details view_** in which all the files/folders are listed with associated details such as Date modified, Type, size etc. You can customize the view to suit your requirements. To customize File Explorer view, follow these steps:

1- Open the **View** tab from the File Explorer ribbon.
2- From the **Layout** menu, point on any of the arrangements (i.e. Extra Large Icons, Large Icons etc.) to preview the arrangement.
3- Click to select any of the arrangements. In the following figures, I have pointed to List and Medium icons to get a preview of the arrangements.

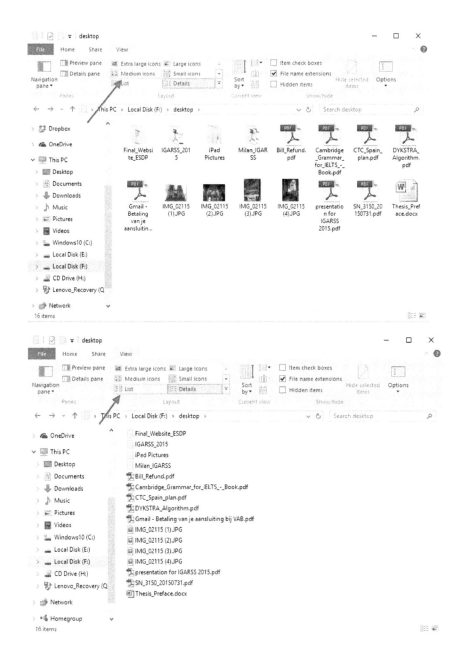

You can also quickly switch between large icon view and detail view using the button located on the bottom right of your File Explorer window. These buttons come in especially handy when the ribbon is unpinned.

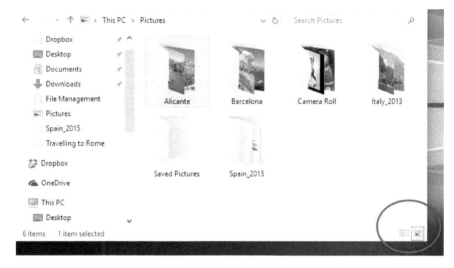

Adding Columns

When you opt to display files and folders in *details view* all the items inside a folder are listed. With each item, you find associated details such as date modified, type and size displayed in columns. You can add more columns to show additional details. Showing more details can help you find and sort files more quickly. To add more columns to your view, follow these steps:

1- From the **View** tab identify the **Current view** menu.
2- Click on **Add Columns**
3- Select the information you want to be displayed in the additional column. For the purpose of demonstration, I am adding a column to show "Date created"

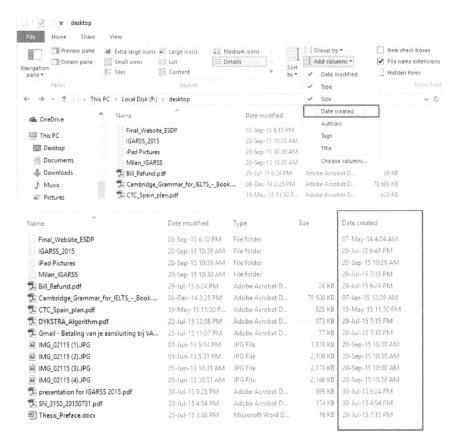

Customizing Panes

Navigation pane displays folder hierarchy in a drive. You can select a folder from the navigation pane to display its contents in the folder pane in File Explorer.

Resizing the Navigation Pane

You can resize the navigation pane so you have more space to show details for every file and folder. To resize the width of navigation pane, move your mouse over the boundary of a folder and navigation pane. The mouse cursor changes to a resize-cursor. Drag toward right/left to resize pane.

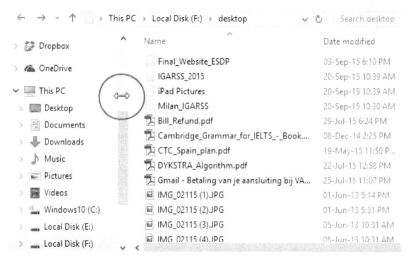

If you feel that the navigation pane takes up a lot of work space you may hide it. To hide the navigation pane follow these steps:

1- In the File Explorer, open the **View** tab
2- Identify the **Navigation Pane** button on the **Panes** menu
3- Click on the **Navigation Pane** button. By default the navigation pane is set to "show" and a small tick appears beside the **Navigation pane**. Clicking on the **Navigation Pane** button will toggle its status. Once you click on it, the navigation pane will hide and the small tick will disappear. You can make it visible again, simply by clicking on it.

Preview Pane

The Preview pane enables you to skim the contents of a file without opening it. To enable the preview pane follow these steps:

1- In the File Explorer open the **View** tab
2- Identify **Preview Pane** button on the **Panes** menu
3- Click on the **Preview Pane**. An additional pane will appear on the right side of the folders pane. Select any file to preview it in the preview pane.

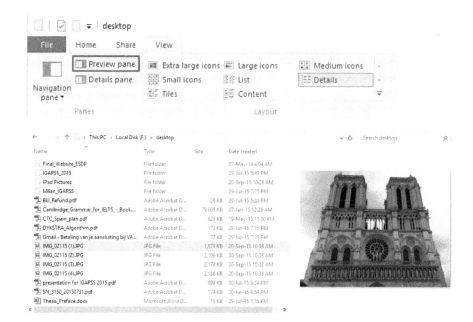

Showing Libraries

Windows 10 provides libraries which collect data from various folders and displays them in a single place. By default they are hidden. You can show libraries by:

1- In the File Explorer open the **View** tab
2- Identify the **Navigation Pane** button on the **Panes** menu
3- Click on the **Navigation Pane** button.
4- Click on **Show Libraries**

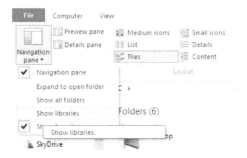

Sorting and Grouping Files/Folders

Sorting and grouping files can help you reach your desired content quickly. Let's explore the sorting and group features in the File Explorer. In the **View** tab, identify the **Current View** menu. Here you have a number of sorting and grouping options. Click on the **Sort by** button and choose the factor according to which you want to sort files. You can sort files according to name, type, size, title, date created etc. If you choose to sort items by **Name:** all the items will be alphabetically ordered.

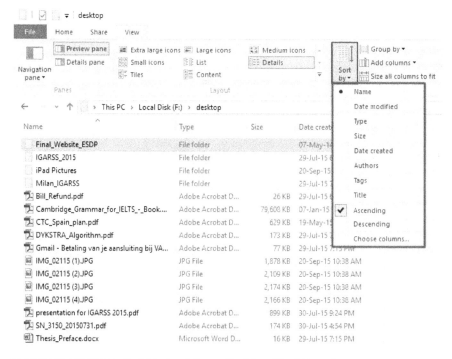

You can also sort items in the folder by clicking on the titles of the folder columns.

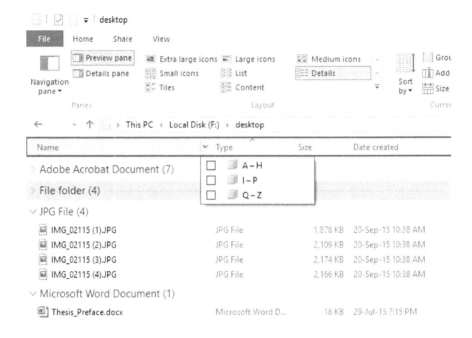

Besides sorting, you can also group files according to a chosen property. To group items in a folder click on the **Group by** button in the **Current View** menu, located on the **View** tab. You can group items by name, type, size, title, date created etc. For this example let's group items by **Type**. All the files and folder are sorted and grouped with a title indicating the type of files. I can also hide/show groups to focus my attention on required types of files.

Name	Type	Size	Date created
› Adobe Acrobat Document (7)			
› File folder (4)			
∨ JPG File (4)			
IMG_02115 (1).JPG	JPG File	1,878 KB	20-Sep-15 10:38 AM
IMG_02115 (2).JPG	JPG File	2,109 KB	20-Sep-15 10:38 AM
IMG_02115 (3).JPG	JPG File	2,174 KB	20-Sep-15 10:38 AM
IMG_02115 (4).JPG	JPG File	2,166 KB	20-Sep-15 10:38 AM

Show/Hide File Extensions

Like file icons, file extensions are also specific for every type of file. By default, the file extensions are hidden. To hide or show a file extension follow these steps:

1- Open the **View** tab in the File Explorer Ribbon.
2- Identify the **File name extension** checkbox in **Show/Hide menu**
3- Check the checkbox to enable the file extension to be visible.

What is a file Extension?

If set to *show extension*, the file name followed by a dot (.) and a set of letters. These are called file extensions. File extensions determine the type of extension, which is used to refer to the proper program for opening the file. Sometimes it's important to know about the file extension. For example you may download a malicious executable file from the internet, assuming it to be an eBook (called something like myebook.pdf.exe); since windows hides the file extension, you will not know that the file is executable (and has an .exe extension) and you may attempt to run it.

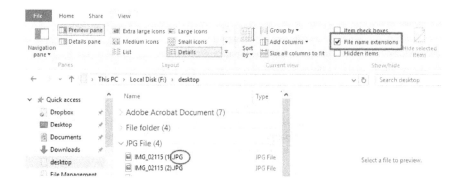

Chapter 10
SEARCHING WITH CORTANA

Cortana, in comparison to Apple's Siri, is a voice controlled digital assistant which first appeared on Windows Phone. Widows 10 enhances Cortana and integrates it into the PC. This chapter explores the potentials of Cortana.

What is Cortana?

Cortana is a unified tool to search the internet and the PC, and also assist users in their everyday tasks. Cortana's functionalities can be distinctly divided as:

1- **Search tool:** You can use Conrtana to search for a file or folder on your PC or to search the internet for specific queries.

2- **Personal Assistant:** Cortana can interact with you like a personal assistant. Cortana, if allowed, gathers data about your internet searches and browsing history and suggests stories and news which may interest you. Cortana can also remind you about appointments, manage your calendar and events, perform quick internet searches, give you an up to date weather report, or just chat with you! Since Cortana is voice controlled, you can issue voice commands to accomplish certain tasks.

Setting up Cortana

To set up Cortana as a personal assistant you need to sign in with a Microsoft account. You may also choose to login to Windows using a local account and only set up Cortana with Microsoft account.

To launch Cortana, simply click on the search bar besides the Start Button. If you are launching Cortana for the first time it will walk you through its features. Click **Next.** Since Cortana interacts with you as a personal assistant it requires you to input your name. Once you provide your name, Cortana will interact with you in a conversational way. During set up you have to allow Cortana to access to your internet and PC usage patterns. As Cortana records and learns about your interests and usage it will be able to give you a more personalized assistance.

After setting up Cortana, the search field label changes from "Search the web and Windows" to "Ask me anything."

Once you have set Cortana, you can customize it. While Cortana will learn about your PC usage with time and develop a database; you can manually add your interests through Notebook.

The Interface

Cortana opens in a vertical panel like Start Menu. The menu is placed on the left-hand side of the vertical panel.

Home ← 🏠

Notebook ← 📓

Reminder ← 💡

Feedback ← 🗨

Here you'll see the latest on what I'm tracking for you. You can see what I've learned in the Notebook, or add things that interest you.

- **Home**: The Home panel displays news updates, weather forecasts, recommendations for eateries, show times and movie trailers, up-to-date flight status', travel tips, traffic routes etc. All the updates displayed in the *Home* panel are customizable. The home panel updates over the internet to get the most recent content according to your interest.
- **Notebook**: The Notebook maintains all your settings in Cortana's database. From the Notebook menu you can customize what Cortana displays in the home-feed. You can also access a number of Cortana settings from here. We will further explore Cortana settings later in this chapter.
- **Reminders**: You can set quick reminders from the reminders menu in Cortana. Cortana reminds you about your up-coming tasks by prompting you with notifications. We will discuss settings and dismissing reminders later on in this chapter.
- **Feedback**: You can send feedback about the functionality of Cortana to Microsoft from this menu.

Personalizing Cortana

To get the best out of Cortana you must introduce yourself to Cortana. Add a list of your interests and details about the type of content you want Cortana to fetch for you. Cortana maintains all your data and activities in a *notebook*. You may add/remove preferences from the notebook to personalize Cortana. Open the **Notebook** pane by clicking on notebook icon from the left-menu.

Adding/Removing Interests

Cortana populates your home feed with news and updates based on your interests. You can add/remove interests in your notebook.

1- Open Cortana
2- Open **Notebook**
3- In Settings, you will find list of interests. You can set preferences for each interest by clicking on them. For the purpose of demonstration, let's add news to interests. Open the News interest and toggle the switches as per your requirement. I will turn the switch for news on. Refresh the home pane of Cortana to see the changes in action.

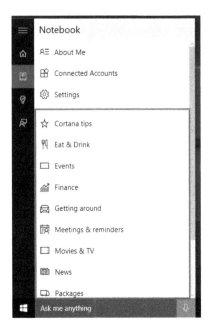

Alternatively, you can hide a specific update in your home-feed and Cortana will automatically remove that interest. To remove an interest from the Home feel follow these steps:

1- In the home feed, identify **...** appearing on the top-right of the story.

2- Click**...**to edit the interest settings.

3- Click **Hide <interest type>**. Cortana will immediately remove the story/card and will update your interests in its database.

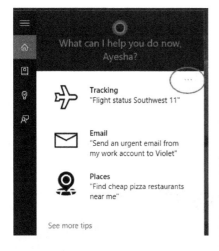

Adding favorite locations

Cortana helps you arrive on your favorite locations on time by giving you traffic conditions and suggestions about the best times to leave. To enable Cortana to help you, you need to add favorite places and traffic as your interest. Let's see how you can do that:

4- Open Cortana
5- Open **Notebook**
6- Click on **About me.** Click on the **Edit Favorites** button in favorite places. Start typing the address of the place you want to save. Cortana will prompt you with suggestions. Select appropriate suggestion.
7- Click on the small save button on the bottom-right. The place will be saved as favorite.
8- Next you need to add **Travel** in your interests, as indicated in previous section. With that set you can rely on Cortana to help you in getting to your favorite places on time.

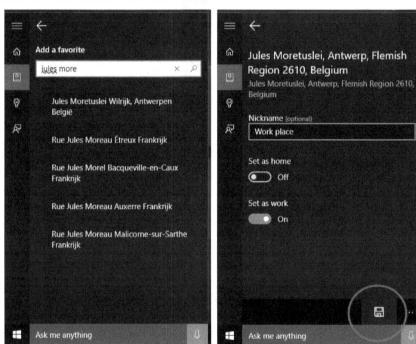

Cleaning Memory

You can wipe the data Cortana has learned about you by following these steps:

1- Open Cortana
2- Open **Notebook**
3- Go to **Settings**
4- Toggle the switch for ***Cortana can give you...*** this cleans Cortana's memory

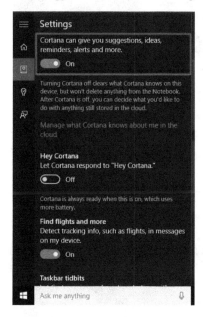

Setting Reminders in Cortana

You can set quick reminders in Cortana from the reminders menu and Cortana will notify you at a set time. To set a quick reminder in Cortana, follow these steps:

1- Open Cortana
2- Open **Reminder** menu
3- Click on the **+** sign located on the bottom right of the vertical pane to add a new reminder.
4- Add a reminder and set a time for the reminder. You will receive a notification from Cortana at the set time. You can also set a reminder to contact a person and add contact details of the **Person** from People (contacts) app or reminder to leave a place an add details of said **Place**.
5- When Cortana reminds you with a notification, you can snooze it or mark it as complete.

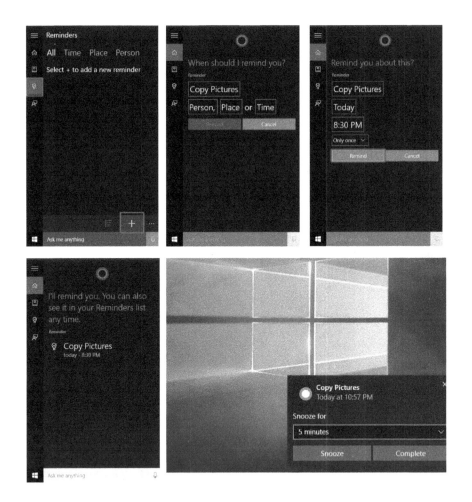

Upcoming reminders can be assessed by following these steps:

1- Open Cortana
2- Open **Reminder** menu

3- Click **All** to display list of upcoming reminders. You can manage individual reminders by clicking on the 🔲 button on the bottom right corner. You can mark the reminders complete or delete them altogether.

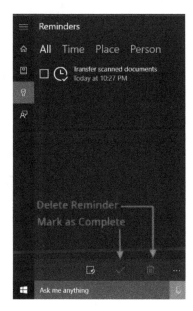

Accessing Reminders from the past

All the reminders which you set in Cortana can be accessed via the History button. To access the list of all the reminders follow these steps;

1- Open Cortana
2- Open **Reminder** menu
3- Identify and click on the **...** icon on bottom right. Click on **History**. The pane populates with list of all past reminders.

Searching with Cortana

Cortana integrates search tools which allows you to fetch content from your PC and on the web simultaneously.

Searching the PC

You can use Cortana to search for files and folders on your PC. To search for a file, simply add a relevant query in the search field. Cortana will search in real-time as you type populating the pane with results from your disk and listing popular internet search queries containing your search term.

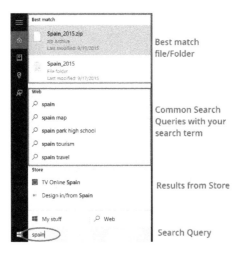

If your required files/folders are listed in the **Best matches** section then you can simply click on the files/folders to open them.

However, if you want to conduct a detailed search, where Cortana will look for the search term within the content then you need to do the following.

1- Type your search term in the search field.
2- Click on **My Stuff**

Cortana will search your OneDrive, photos and folders on your disk to search for files which contain the search term within its content. Let's investigate closely. I have searched for the term **Spain**. Cortana populates the search results according to file type. The first result comes from OneDrive. As you can see, the file title does not contain the search term, however "Spain" is contained within its content. Also Cortana populates all photos from various destinations and presents it in form of grid.

To open destination folder containing your required file right-click any search result and click on open file location.

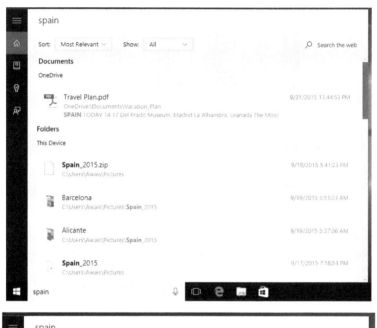

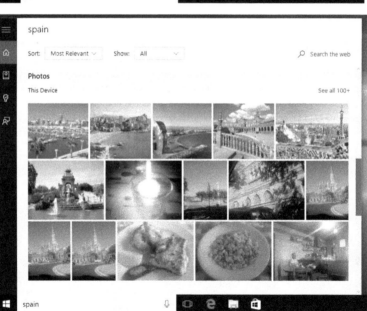

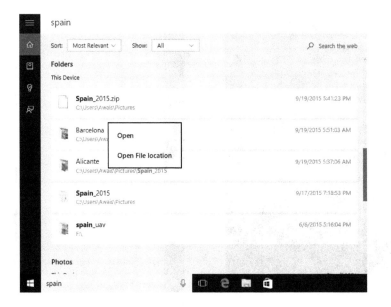

Cortana uses Bing's search engine to fetch the internet for your search term. To search the web for your search term:

1- Type your search term in the search field.
2- Click on **Web**

This opens a Bing search results page for your search term in the Microsoft Edge Browser. You can also click on any of the popular search queries including your search term to open Bing search results for that particular query.

Natural language Commands

Cortana can process your natural language commands. Put simply, you can talk to Cortana, ask questions just like you would talk to a friend. While Cortana has voice recognition built in, you may also use the search field to type in your questions.

 If your PC has a microphone built in you can talk to Cortana, dictate emails, give voice commands and ask question instead of typing in the search field. You may also perform searches by speaking out your search terms. If you find yourself frequently giving voice commands to Cortana, then you may want to configure Cortana to respond to "hey Cortana". If set, whenever you say "hey Cortana", Cortana will be prompted to assist you automatically.

SECTION 5
WORKING WITH APPS

Chapter 11

THE MAIL APP

Windows 10 comes bundled with number of useful apps. It's important to invest the time to learn the basics of the productivity apps as it will boost your output immensely. We will restrict our discussion to the Mail app, People and Calendar apps, which are by far the most extensively used apps. These apps work together.

Accounts Set up for Mail, People and Calendar

Windows 10 comes with a built-in Mail application which enables you to send and receive emails directly from your PC. If you are logged in your PC with your Microsoft account, by default your Mail app manages emails from your email account associated to your Microsoft account. On the contrary, if you are logged in your PC through a local account then you will have to setup Mail app with your email.

You can set up the Mail app with multiple accounts and have emails from accounts other than Microsoft Outlook email. This frees you from the hassle of having many service specific eMail apps and accounts. Also, since Mail app is integrated into Windows 10, you are able to see new email notifications in **Live Tiles**, in the Start Menu or email notifications in the locked screen. All these offerings make the Mail app your all-in-one app for mail-management.

When you add accounts to your Mail app, associated contact lists and calendars will synchronize with **People** and **Calendar app** automatically.

 When you set up accounts with Mail app, contacts and calendars from the Mail app automatically synchronizes with People and Calendar. However this is not true for all accounts. For example, iCloud will allow you to synchronize, but Yahoo does not offer this feature.

Setting up Mail app

When you launch the Mail app for the first time, it displays a Welcome note and will require you to set it up. You can use the Mail app with multiple accounts and with services other than Outlook or Hotmail. My Mail app is already setup with my Hotmail account since I have logged into my PC using my Microsoft account. For the purpose of demonstration, let's add another account.

1- Click on the **Get Started** button on the Mail app launch screen.
2- Click on the **Add account** button to add another account in Mail app. A pop-up window appears with a list of common email-account services. Select your email service provider.
3- Provide **Email** and **Password** for that email account. Click on **Sign-in**.
4- Provide a **Name** for that account. You will be using this name when sending emails.
5- Click **Done** and you are now setup with the built-in Mail app! You may continue to add as many email accounts as you need. You may also opt to add an account later.

Launch the Mail app by clicking on the **Ready to go** button.

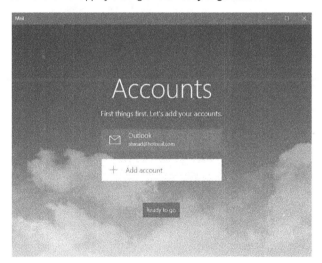

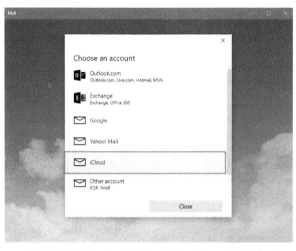

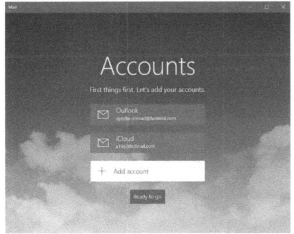

The Mail app comprises of two panes; the Navigation Pane and the Mail Pane. Select the folder from your email account in the navigation pane to view emails in that folder. The Mail app defaults to the "Inbox" folder of your email account and shows all your emails in chronological order.

Navigation Pane → Mail Pane →

Calendar   Settings

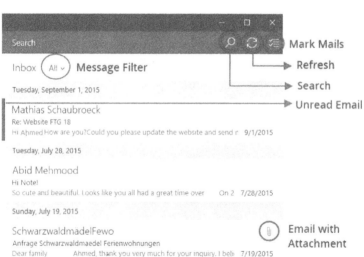

Mark Mails

Message Filter

Refresh

Search

Unread Email

Email with
Attachment

You can also add accounts to your Mail app later, when your Mail app is completely set up. Adding email accounts is discussed later in this chapter.

Mail app Basics

Switching Accounts

If you have set up your Mail app with multiple accounts you have to switch between accounts to see emails from the different accounts. To switch accounts follow these steps:

1- In the navigation pane click on **Accounts**.
2- A vertical pane appears on the right of the navigation pane, listing all the accounts you have set up with the Mail app.
3- Click to select any of your email accounts to view mails received by that account.

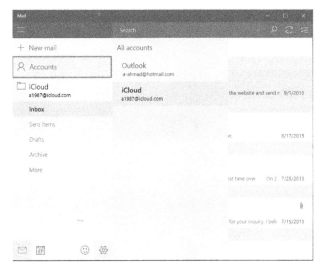

Composing Emails

The account you have selected from the Accounts button is your active account. You can compose and send email from that account by following these steps:

1- Click on **+ New Mail** on the top of the navigation pane.

2- Compose an email. Start typing the name of recipient and the Mail app will suggest contacts either from your address book (called People app on Windows 10) or email-address which you have recently contacted. Add a subject and email content.

3- You may also use limited formatting in your email provided in the Format menu.

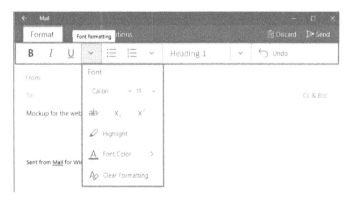

Attaching Files

You can attach files and zipped folders in your emails. To attach files:

1- Click on the **Insert** tab.

2- Click on **Attach** to browse file/zipped folder from your computer. Alternatively, if you want to attach a photo select **Picture**. Clicking on the **Picture** button opens the Pictures folder on your PC. Select your required file. Your chosen file will be attached in the email.

3- For image attachments, you have number of different options in the **Pictures** tab. Select the image to open the **Pictures** tab. From here you may rotate, crop or resize an image. You may also provide an alternative text, just in case the image fails to load on the receiver's end.

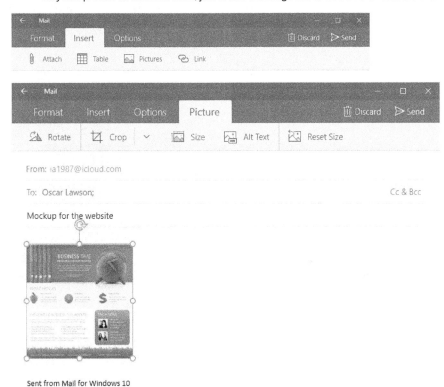

Sent from Mail for Windows 10

Adding Multiple Recipients

You can send an email to different people at the same time. Simply type the email address of multiple recipients, separated by; in the **To:** text field. As you type the recipient's name/email, the Mail app automatically begins to suggests contacts. If correct, you can click the suggestion and the name/email address will be added to the **To:** field with; at the end. You can continue to type name/email-address of more recipients. The list of contacts added in **To:** is visible to all the recipients. You can also use CC (carbon copy) and Bcc (Blind carbon copy) fields.

Sending Email

Once you have composed the email you can send it from the app using the SEND button on the top-right.

Read, Reply & Forward

The Message Pane displays a list of email headers, showing the name of sender, the subject and a limited preview of the email itself. You can click on the email header to open and read the complete email.

- **Reply:** To reply (send email in response/reply) to an email, click on the **reply** button on the top-menu.
- **Reply All**: Reply to all the recipients by clicking **Reply All**
- **Forward:** You can forward or pass the email on to another person in your contact list.
- **Archive:** You can archive emails to access them at later time.
- **Delete:** Moves the email to the deleted messages folder.
- **Mark as Unread:** You might want to mark an email as unread, so you can return to it at a later time. To mark an email unread click on **...** button beside **Set Flag** and click on **Mark as Unread**

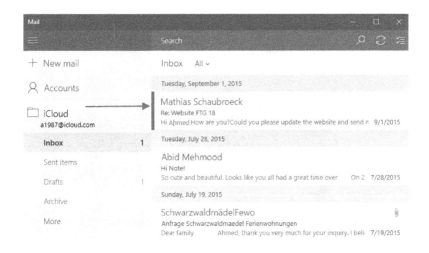

 We have seen that an email can be sent to multiple recipients. When replying, you may choose to send an email to the email sender alone (**Reply**), or to send a reply to all recipients of the email (**Reply All**).

Flagging Emails

When you need to reference an email quite a few times you can flag it. Flagged emails are represented with icons making them prominent and easy to spot as you return. In Outlook, flagged emails appear above new emails.

You can flag emails in the Mail app using the following methods:

1- Point your mouse to the email header in the message pane. Two icons appear; both the icons are self-explanatory. Use the left –trashcan icon to delete and/or right flag icon to flag email.

2- In the message pane, click to open message. Select **Set Flag**.

 All the changes (mark email as read, flag email, delete email etc.) you do in your Mail app will be reflected across all your accounts. For example if you flag an email received in an iCloud account from Mail app, the email will be flagged when you access your iCloud account on the internet or on your idevice.

Going Back

Once you have opened an email to read, you can go back to all messages by clicking on the back icon on the top-right.

Changing Signature

An email signature is a phrase which is appended to your email messages automatically. By default, the email signature is turned on and is set to "**Sent from Mail for Windows 10**". When you compose email using the Mail app, the signature is appended at the end of email. To change or to turn off the signature, follow these steps:

1- Click on the gear button to open the **Settings** pane.
2- Click on **Options**
3- Scroll down to **Signature.** To modify the signature edit the signature text field. Or to disable signature completely toggle the switch off. You may use your name and contact details as signature.

Managing Accounts Settings

From the Settings in Mail app you can manage settings for individual mail accounts. To go to settings, identify the small gear button on the bottom-right of the navigation pane.

1- Click on the gear button to open **Settings** pane.
2- Click on **Accounts**. A list of all the accounts you have set up with Mail app will pop-up.
3- Select an account to manage its settings.

Let's look at the settings available for your email account. For every mail account you have:

1- **Account settings**: Account settings present options for changing email, password or deleting the account from within your Mail app.
2- **Mailbox Sync Settings**: You can control email synchronization, options for downloading emails, and sender name options from here.
   - **Download New Email**: This setting tells the Mail app how often you want to download new emails. By default it is set to "based on my use" i.e. Windows will analyze your usage patterns for this account and set the time period for you to reduce the data and conserve the battery. You may change the setting manually by clicking on the drop down menu and selecting a specific time duration. Selecting, let's say 15 minutes, means that Mail app will check every 15 minutes for new emails in that account and download any new emails automatically.

- **Download Emails from**: This setting tells the Mail app the time frame for which you want to download and retrieve mails. By default the setting is set to the last 3 months. Mail older than months 3 months are deleted automatically.
- **Sync Options**: Lastly, from here you can control if you want to sync contacts and calendars with associated Microsoft apps, namely People and Calendar. You can toggle the individual switch to turn/on off sync.

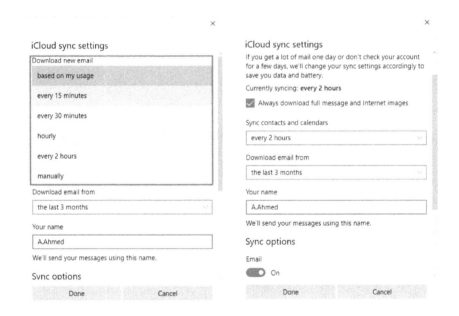

How to Conserve Data?

To get the most out of your battery and efficiently use data, you may choose to:

1- Uncheck "**Always download full messages and internet images**"
2- Set **Download new emails** to manually. You may then choose to download new emails whenever you choose (on-the-fly, or in other words, when you check your email).

Adding Email Accounts

We have seen setting up accounts in addition to a Microsoft account with Mail app as we set up the app. However, adding accounts can be done anytime i.e. even after setting up the Mail app. To add an account to Mail app, follow these steps:

1- Click on the gear button to open **Settings** pane.

2- Click on **Accounts**. A list of all the accounts you have set up with the Mail app will pop-up.

3- Click on **Add account**. Follow the process step-by-step.

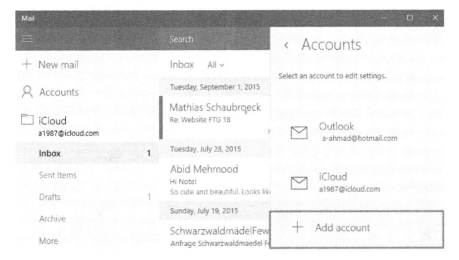

Chapter 12
WORKING WITH CALENDAR APP

Adding email accounts to Mail app automatically synchronizes associated contacts and calendars with the **People** and **Calendar app**. When you will first launch the Calendar app you will be greeted with the same Welcome screen, seen while setting up Mail app. However, this time, you will find that account listing includes the account you already set up with the Mail app. In my case, I see an Outlook account, associated to my Microsoft account I use for logging into my PC and my iCloud account, which I added while setting up Mail app. The Calendar app automatically synchronizes the calendar associated to my iCloud account.

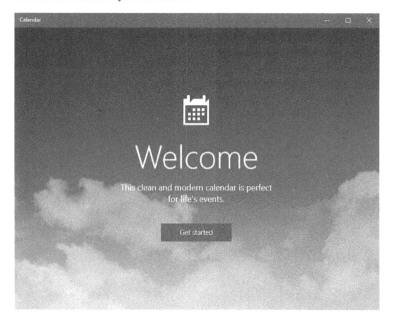

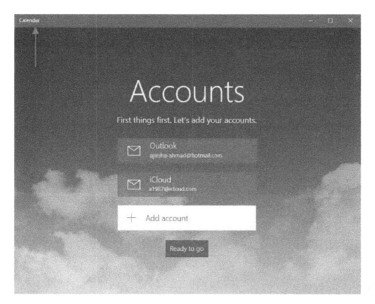

The Calendar app shows events from all your associated calendars with color coding for easy comprehension.

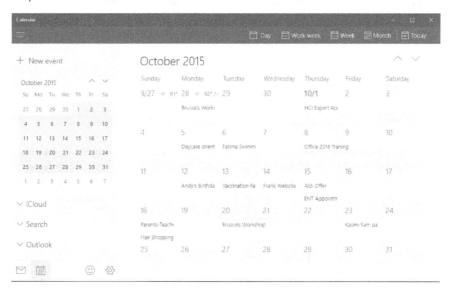

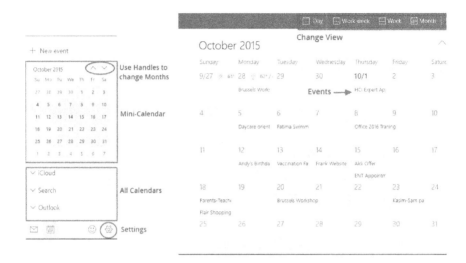

Calendar View & Settings

Hiding/Showing Calendar

For every account you may have one or more calendars. To view calendars associated to an account use the left-arrow beside account title to expand and collapse the list of associated calendars.

Each calendar is assigned a color, so you may understand the nature of events by merely glancing at your calendar. The following figure shows three calendars from my iCloud account, namely Work Agenda, Children and Home. You may choose to show appointments from only select calendars. In the following figure, since all the calendars for the iCloud account are checked, events and appointments from each of the calendars are showing in the *month* view.

☐ Day 🗔 Work week ☐ Week ▦ Month ⊞ Today

+ New event

October 2015

∧ ∨

October 2015					∧ ∨	
Su	Mo	Tu	We	Th	Fr	Sa
27	28	29	30	1	2	3
4	5	6	7	8	9	10
11	12	13	14	15	16	17
18	19	20	21	22	23	24
25	26	27	28	29	30	31
1	2	3	4	5	6	7

∧ iCloud

☑ Work Agenda

☑ Children

☑ Home

✉ 🗓 ☺ ⚙

Sunday	Monday	Tuesday	Wednesday	Thursday	Friday	Saturday
9/27 ☀ 61°	28 ☀ 62°/·	29	30	10/1	2	3
	Brussels Works			HCI Expert App		
4	5	6	7	8	9	10
	Daycare orient	Fatima Swimm		Office 2016 Traning		
11	12	13	14	15	16	17
	Andy's Birthda	Vaccination Fa	Frank Website	Aldi Offer		
				ENT Appointr		
18	19	20	21	22	23	24
Parents-Teach		Brussels Workshop			Kasim-Sam pa	
Flair Shopping						
25	26	27	28	29	30	31

To view events and appointments from only selected calendars, check required calendar and leave the rest unchecked. In the following figure, I have chosen to show events and appointments from only my Children's calendar.

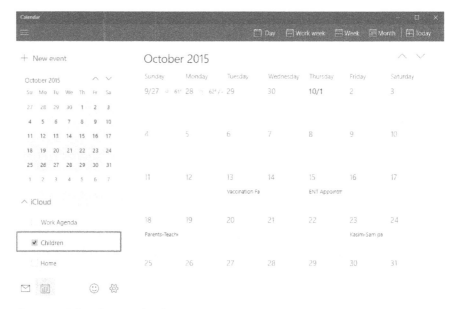

Changing Color for a Calendar

Color coding your calendars can help you understand the nature of appointments at a glance. To change the color of a calendar:

1- Right-click on the calendar.
2- Select color from set of colors in the pop- menu

Changing View

When working with the Calendar app you may find it useful to switch calendar views to show appointments from day, week or month to keep yourself more focused. You can switch between views using the menu on top.

Selecting month view gives you an overview of your schedule for an entire month. You may also select month from the mini-calendar on the left-hand pane. Likewise selecting day (or multiple days) gives you schedule for the selected day. The following figure shows appointments for two days. The appointments are shown for every hour.

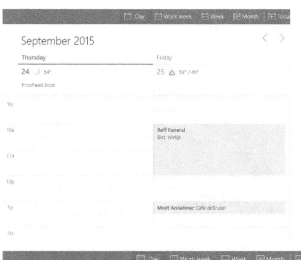

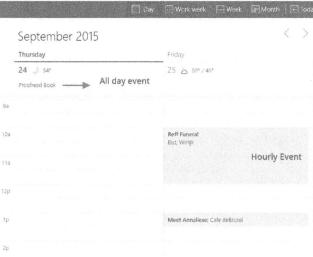

Tile for Calendar app in the Start Menu is a *Live Tile*. You can view appointments for the day without even having to open the app!

Setting Work Week and Working Hours

When changing views you might have observed "Work week"; a view which shows appoints by work week. By default, work week is set from Monday to Friday. You can set your work week, first day of week and working hours to suit your requirements from the calendar settings.

1- Click on the gear icon on the bottom right to open Settings.
2- Click on **Calendar settings**
3- A check list of days appears under ***Days in Work week***. Check or uncheck checkboxes displayed with each day to alter your week as required.
4- From the same pane you can change ***First Day of Week*** and ***Working Hours***

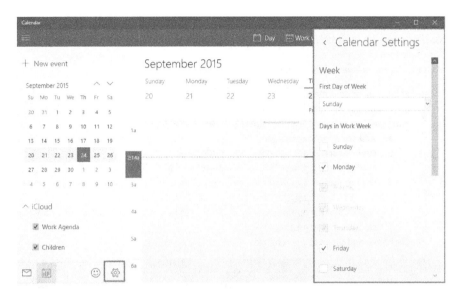

Basics of the Calendar app

Viewing Appointments

To view an appointment, point your mouse over the event. The event details will be displayed in an overlay window. You can click on **More details** to view further information about the event.

Creating Appointment

The Calendar app enables you to create appointment in a number of ways.

1- Click to select a date In which you want to create an appointment.
2- Add details for the event in pop-up box.
3- Click **Done** to save the appointment

 When creating an appointment in month view, the event time defaults to **All day**. On the other hand, if you are viewing your calendar in week/day view, you can click on a specific time frame to set an appointment for the selected time.

Alternately, you can also click on the **+ New Event** button to create event.

Once you have quickly created an event you can edit the appointment and add helpful details about the event such as location, event description, set reminders for the event or invite one of your contacts. To edit an event to add details, follow these steps:

1- Point to an appointment.
2- Click **More details** in the overlay box
3- A detailed view of event is shown where you can:
   a. **Add Location:** Set location
   b. **Event description:** Add notes about the event.
   c. **Modify time:** Uncheck "All day" and select time from dropdown boxes.
   d. **Set Reminder:** If you want to be reminded about the event, you may set a reminder from the Reminder drop-down box on top. By default it is set to 15 minutes. This implies that the app will notify you 15 minutes before the event occurs. You may also set the event to repeat.
4- Click **Save and Close** to save changes

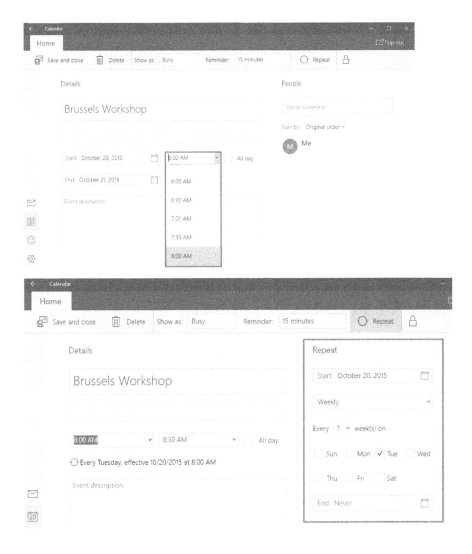

The following figure shows a weekly event occurring every Tuesday from 8:00 AM.

ve and close   🗑 Delete   Show as: Busy   Reminder: 15 minutes   ↻ Repeat   🔒

Details

Vitamin D |

Location

| 8:00 AM ⌄ | 8:30 AM ⌄ | All day |

↻ Every 3 weeks on Tuesday, effective 9/24/2015 from 8:00 AM to 8:30 AM

❋ Home   ⌄

Event description

Repeat

Start: September 24, 2015   🗓

Weekly   ⌄

Every   3 ⌄ week(s) on

| Sun | Mon | ✓ Tue | Wed |
| Thu | Fri | Sat | |

End: Never   🗓

If you set your lock screen to display notifications from the Calendar app, then you can see your reminders even outside the Calendar app from the lock screen!

Chapter 13

WORKING WITH PEOPLE APP

People app is the address book app for Windows 10. Contacts from email accounts you set up with Mail app will be synchronized and displayed in People app. You can lunch the People app from the Start Menu -> All Apps. Note the following figure, as I have set up my iCloud account in addition to my Outlook account in Mail app. The People app aggregates and lists contacts from my iCloud account and my Outlook account.

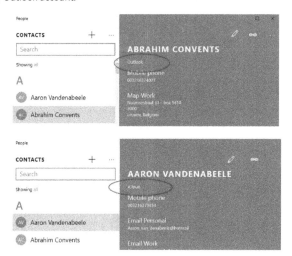

Filtering Contacts

By default, the People app displays contacts from your all your accounts. However you may filter contacts to display contact cards from select account only. To do so follow these steps:

1- Identify **Showing all** link under the Search field located on top of the right pane. Note "all" appears as a clickable link.
2- Click *all.* Check to select the accounts from which you want to show on contact cards.

Alternatively

1- Click on the **...** button to access Settings.
2- Scroll down in the Settings window to **Show contacts from**
3- Select accounts by clicking on check boxes besides each account.

You may also hide contacts cards for which the phone number is unavailable. To hide contact cards, identify the option "*Hide contacts without phone numbers*"; toggle switch to turn this option on or off. This option filters the address book and only displays contacts which can be called or texted.

Adding Contact

To add a contact to any of your account from the People app follow these steps:

1- Click on the **+** button on top of contact list.
2- Select Account: You will be promoted to select the account where you want to save the contact.
3- Add contact details such as name, phone number, and personal email.
   a. To add Name details such as Surname, First name, Title etc. click on the small pen icon (edit icon) beside the name field. Add details in the required field.
   b. To add additional contact information, such as work email and address, click on **+Email** and **+Address**. Select to add field from the pop-up window and add related detail.
   c. Likewise, to add additional contact details such as job title, position, birthday etc. click on **+Others**, select the field from the Add Field popup menu to add in contact card. Add details.
   d. To add a photo to your contact card, click on **Add Photo** in a circle provided on the top of contact card. This will open your photo library with large image previews arranged in chronological order. Select image you want to assign to a contact. Choose a circular selection from the image by dragging handles to adjust selection. Click a tick icon to save selection and assign image.
4- Click Floppy **(Save)** icon to save the contact card

People

CONTACTS   **+**   ...

Search

Showing all

Choose account

Choose an account and we'll save your
new contacts there from now on. You'll
always have the option to use a different
account whenever you add a contact.

Outlook

iCloud

Close

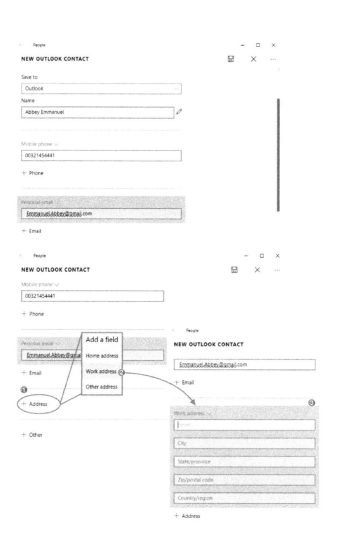

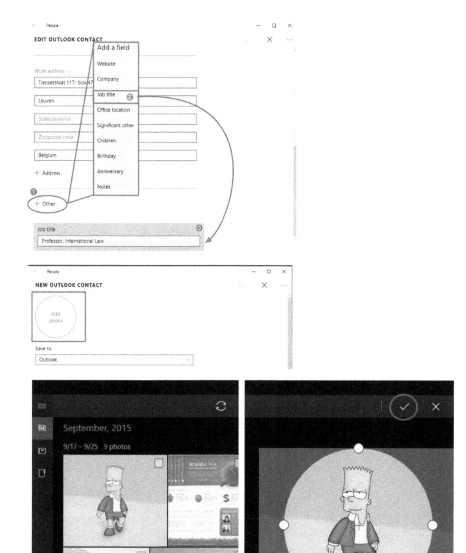

Edit Card

Once you have created a contact you, you can edit it anytime. To **Edit** a contact card select the contact from the left-pane and click on pen/edit icon on top-right.

Changing Account for Saving contact

When creating a contact for the first time, the People app prompts you to provide the location where you would like to save the contact card. Every time it uses the account selected for the first time to save a newly created contact, you can change the account preference by:

1- When creating a contact identify the **Save to** Drop-down menu
2- Click to open the drop-down menu, listing associated accounts. Select account of choice.

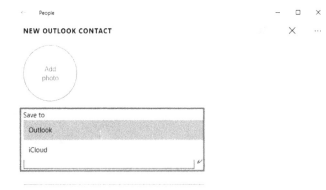

Deleting contact

To delete a contact, select the contact from the left-pane and click on **...** icon on top-right. Select Delete contact from the drop-down menu to delete it

Sharing Contact Card

To delete a contact, select the contact from the left-pane and click on ••• icon on top-right. Select Share Contact from the drop-down menu. Click on the **tick** button to confirm the action. A list of apps installed on your system that support contact sharing will appear in an overlay window on right. Select the app from the list which you would like to use for sharing contacts. I will use the Mail app to mail (share) the contact details. This generates an email with contact attachment.

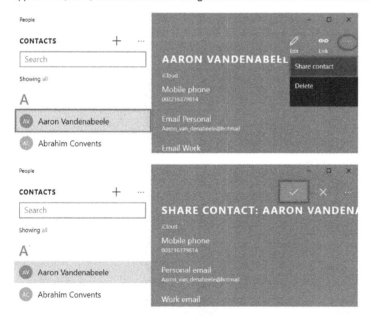

From: ahmad@hotmail.com

To: | Cc & Bcc

Contact information for Aaron Vandenabeele

Attachments

Aaron Vandenabeele.vcf
290 bytes

Sending email from People app

The Mail, Calendar and People app work together. You can send emails to your contacts directly from the People app. To email contact from the People app;

1- Select the contact to email.
2- Click on their email address. This opens a pop-up box prompting you to select the app you would like to use for mailing the selected contact.
3- Select your required app to send email. For this example I am using the Windows 10 Mail app to send email to the selected contact

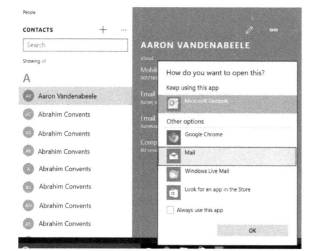

Chapter 14

WINDOWS 10 APPS ROUND UP

Windows 10 bundles apps in various categories, ranging from weather, productivity, communication to cloud storage. In previous chapters we have seen OneDrive app for cloud storage, Mail, People and Calendar app. This chapter discusses other useful apps that come bundled with Windows 10.

Apps for browsing the internet

Windows 10 introduces a brand new web browser, **Microsoft Edge**, which is its default browser. The new browser is fast and more reliable. You can launch Edge Browser from the Task Bar or from the Start Menu. Microsoft combines the goodies provided by third party plugins such as Reader, Readability, Read-it-Later etc. and integrates it in its new browser, Edge. Note the distinct new features of browser:

1- **Reading mode:** When viewing a webpage you are often interrupted by advertisements and other distracting images. Microsoft Edge Browser's reading mode, cleans the clutter and presents you the content of the article in a neat book-like interface. This helps you focus on content. You can enable reading mode by clicking on the book icon on the top menu. Note that reading mode is not available on every webpage, particularly on web pages which do not have substantial content.

Without Reader Mode	With Reader Mode

2- **Reading list:** You can save web pages for later reference in your Reading list. Unlike Favorites, the reading list is like a to-do list which you must finish. Favorites on the other hand retain your bookmarks.

3- **Ask Cortana right from the browser:** You can ask Cortana to look up words and phrases in a webpage for you. To do so, select and right-click on a word. Select **Ask Cortana** from the context menu.

4- **Annotate and share:** You can open a webpage in annotation mode and add personal notes to it. You can save your annotation and notes on the webpage and share annotated web pages or save them to your reading list. To open the annotation mode, click the pen icon on the top right-corner.

Internet Explorer

Internet Explorer is still available on your PC. To access Internet Explorer, follow these steps:

1- Open the Start Menu->all apps
2- Click on **Windows Accessories**
3- Click **Internet Explorer**

Other apps

Windows 10 also includes the following apps:

- **Alarm Clock:** The Alarm clock app provides clocks for times around the world. It also has the alarm and stop watch feature.
- **Calculator:** A standard Calculator app which you can switch to scientific calculator as well.
- **Camera:** You can use the Camera app to snap a picture with your built-in laptop/tablet camera.
- **Food & Drink:** This app lets you plan your meal and build a grocery shopping list. You can also find recipes from famous chefs.
- **Health & Fitness:** This app can be used to monitor your diet and daily exercise routine.
- **Groove Music:** Access online music stores using this app.
- **Money:** Find real-time finance news with the Money app.
- **Movies & TV:** Access online video store to download videos.
- **Skype**
- **News:** Get real-time news updates based on the location you selected while installing Windows 10.
- **Photos app:** View and edit photos. The Photos app also offers filters for your photos.
- **OneNote:** Note taking app for Windows 10
- **Reader:** This app can be used to open and read files in various formats including TIFF and PDF.
- **Sports:** Access real-time sports news depending upon your location.

- **Xbox:** Use this app to play online game or download and play games on your PC.

Chapter 15
MANAGING APPS

Installing apps from the App Store

There are apps which come pre-installed in Windows 10 such as the Mail, Weather app, Calendar, Map etc. nonetheless, you can also download apps from the Microsoft App Store according to your computing requirements. To download an app from the Windows App Store, follow these steps:

1- Launch **Windows Store** from the Task Bar or Start Menu.
2- You can search for an app or you may browse for an app in Windows Store categories.
   a. **Searching:** Locate the search field in the top-right corner of the window. Search for required app. Search box will guess the name and suggest app. You may also search for categories and the search box will suggest most relevant apps.
   b. **Browsing:** Windows Store also maintains charts such as App Top Charts, Game Top Charts, Featured Apps, Most Popular, and Top Free etc. You may browse through the list and select an app.
   c. **Movies & TV:** You can also select movies and music albums from the store.
3- Apps may be free or may be priced. If you want to purchase an app you must add details of your back account in your Microsoft account details. For the purpose of demonstration, I am downloading a Facebook app which is free. Click on the blue button titled **Free**, to download the app.

4- **Downloads & Updates:** You can access the download and update section by clicking on ↓ (down arrow) icon besides your account name. Here you can check the download status and % complete for apps you are currently downloading. You can also pause downloads from here.

Home   Apps   Games   Music   Movies & TV   Search

StumbleUpon

hop Express   StumbleUpon   NFL Showdown
hance images   Over 500 interests for you to explore   Build yo

App top charts & categories   Game top charts & categories   Featured

Picks for you   Show all

Zip Opener   Disney Infinity: Toy   GS Kids! Toddler   Spider Solitaire 8   Fitbit   Hidden Objects:

Searching for "Productivity"

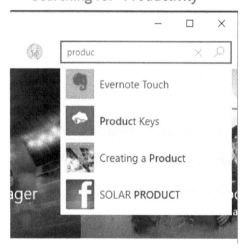

Uninstalling apps

Uninstalling apps which you do not use can free up hard disk space and help you keep a clutter free PC. Apps which surface from the Windows Store can be removed as follows:

1. Identify the tile of the app in the Start Menu. Alternatively find the app in the Start Menu. Right-click on app title.
2. Click Uninstall.

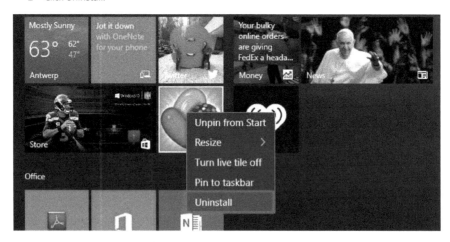

When you attempt to delete Windows Legacy apps or apps which you've downloaded from the web (e.g. Google's Chrome, Mozilla Firefox etc. also called **non-native apps**), the uninstall button re-directs you to the old **Add/Remove** Programs window. You can select the app (or call it program) from the list and click Uninstall from the menu.

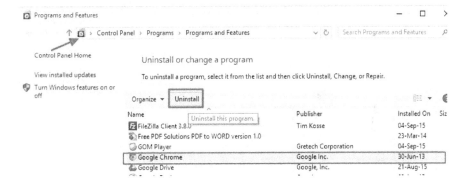

Alternatively,

1- From the Start Menu go to **Settings**
2- Open **System** menu
3- Go to **Apps & Features** and scroll down. Here you will find a list of apps. You can sort each app by name and date. Click on the non-native app you want to remove, this will slide in two options: Move and uninstall. Click Uninstall to remove the app. Try selecting a native (bundled app) you will see that the Uninstall/move option is disabled.

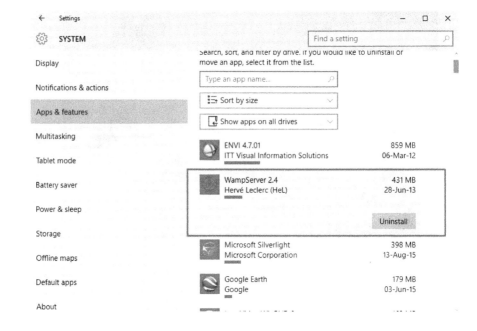

Apps Memory Usage

To investigate the memory occupied by each app on your PC, follow these steps:

1- From the Start Menu go to **Settings**
2- Open **System** menu
3- Go to **Apps & Features** and scroll down to the list of apps. Under each app you will find the %space indicated in a horizontal bar.

From here you can learn how much space an app occupies and you can free up space in case you are running short of storage.

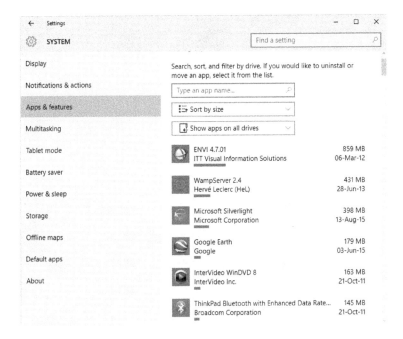

App Permission

To let the app function correctly it needs access to your folders and device components. For example, let's say you download a fancy photo-editing app, it will require access to your photos to work on, add filters etc. To gain access, every app requires permission from you. Likewise, there are a number of social networking apps which require access to your location, photos and camera etc. However, sometimes you might want to monitor and restrict app permissions. To investigate which app has permission for various features follow these steps:

1- From the Start Menu go to **Settings**
2- Open **System** menu
3- Go to **Privacy**. The left hand panel lists various features such as location, camera, calendar etc. Select any of the features to find out which apps have permission to access it. I have selected Microphone in the following figure; Microsoft Edge, Twitter, Xbox and Windows Voice recorder to have access to my microphone as each, the toggle switch is set to ON.

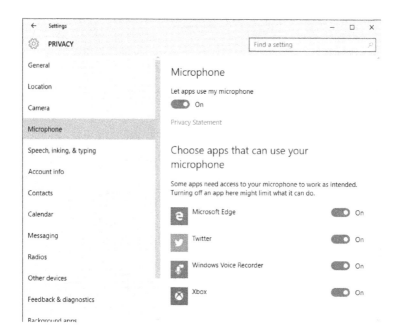

Restricting an App

To **restrict** an app from having access to a certain feature, simply navigate to the feature and toggle the switch OFF for that app. I am restricting Windows Voice Recorder to use my Microphone; to do that I will toggle the switch beside the Windows Voice Recorder to off (for Microphone).

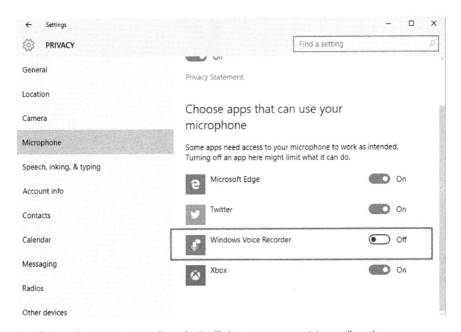

Now if I open the Windows Voice Recorder it will give me an error as it is not allowed to access my microphone.

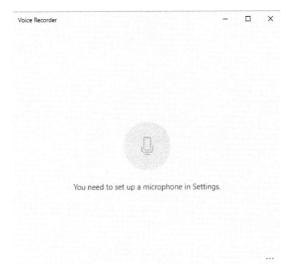

SECTION 6

SYSTEM & USER MANAGEMENT

Chapter 16
ADMINISTRATOR & USER ACCOUNT
MANAGEMENT

In this section we will see how you can manage your administrator account and create and manage multiple User Accounts on your PC. We will also touch on Windows family features.

Managing Administrator Account

Adding image to your Account

To add an image of yourself to your account, follow these steps

1- From the Start Menu Go to **Settings**.
2- Select **Accounts**.
3- Select **Your account.** The window shows your name and your Microsoft email (if you have signed in with your Microsoft account), and your account type. If you do not share your computer then you are by default, the Administrator of your computer. Scroll down and click the **Browse** button in *Your picture* section to select and assign a picture to your account. Alternatively, you can use the camera to take a fresh picture. Windows saves and displays thumbnails of three of your recently changes pictures so you can easily switch between them

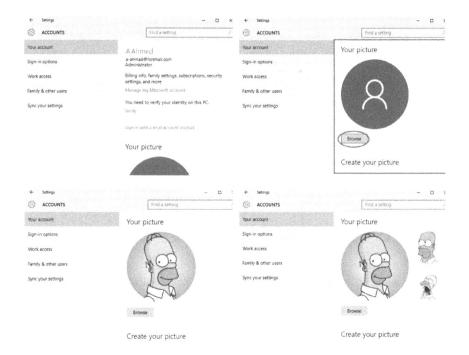

Verifying your Identity

While installing, if you have chosen to use your Microsoft account for singing in your PC, you may need to verify your identity. To verify your identity follow these steps:

1- From Start Menu Go to **Settings**.
2- Select **Accounts**.
3- Select **Your account**. Scroll down and click **Verify** under *You need to verify your identity on this PC*. Microsoft will send a code to the alternative email address (also the recovery email address) you have set up with your main Microsoft account. Once received, type the code into the verify window and click **Next**. You will need to verify your identify, before making any purchase from the Windows App Store.

Changing PIN

If you are signed in your PC using your Microsoft account then chances are, that you have already set up a PIN. A PIN is a short code which you use to sign into your device. Selecting a PIN not only protects your Microsoft account's password but it also facilitates quick sign-in on touch devices as typing 4 digits is easier on touch screens than typing long passwords. To change your PIN, follow these steps:

1- From Start Menu Go to **Settings**.
2- Select **Accounts**.
3- Select **Sign-in Options.**
4- Scroll down to the PIN section and click on the **Change** Button.
5- Type in the old PIN to verify your identity and then type (and repeat) New PIN.

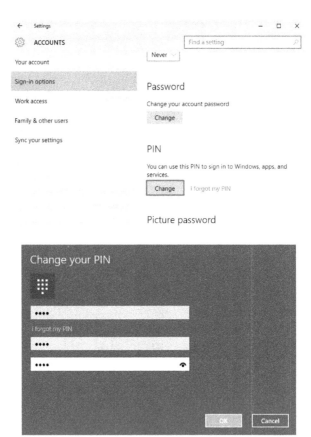

Removing PIN

The alternative to your PIN is your Microsoft account's password. If you choose to remove your PIN from your computer, you will use your Microsoft account's password to sign into your PC. To remove the PIN, follow these steps:

1- From Start Menu Go to **Settings**.
2- Select **Accounts**.
3- Select **Sign-in Options.**
4- Scroll down to the PIN section and click on **I forgot my PIN.** You will have to type your Microsoft account password to confirm resetting your PIN.

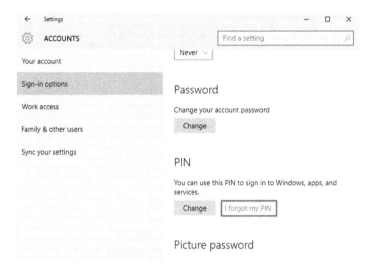

Changing Account Type

Windows 10 allows you to sign-in with your Microsoft account besides local accounts, as discussed in detail in chapter 1. To sign-in with a Microsoft account or a local account is a decision you should make before you begin the Windows 10 installation process, however, it is easy to get baffled. Thankfully, you can always go back and change your account type (refer to Microsoft vs. local account discussion in chapter 1). To discontinue using your Microsoft account and sign-in with a local account follow these steps:

1- From Start Menu Go to **Settings**.
2- Select **Accounts**.
3- Select **Your account.**
4- Identify the option **Sign-in with a local account instead**. Save your work and provide your password to continue.
5- Enter the username and password you would like to use for a local account, Click Next.

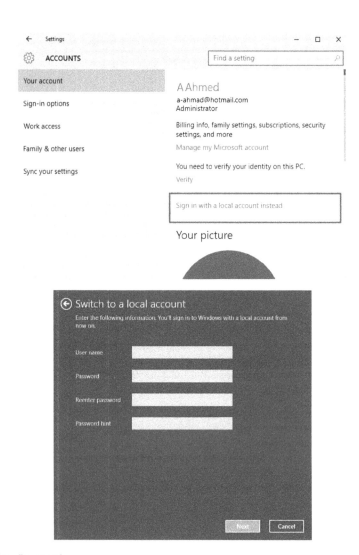

Changing Password

You can change your administrator password. If you are using a Microsoft account to sign in to your PC, then changing the password would change the password for which you use with Microsoft services. If you are using a local account, changing the password will have no effect on your password associated with Microsoft services.

To change your password, follow these steps:

1- From the Start Menu Go to **Settings**.
2- Select **Account**.
3- Select **Sign-in Options.**
4- Scroll down to Password, click **Change** button. If using your Microsoft account, you will need to provide your PIN to confirm your identity.

Managing Multi-User Accounts

Windows 10, like its predecessors is designed to be a multi-user operating system i.e. the computer can be used among many users and each user is able to keep their own set of files, system preferences and settings. You can also set permissions for different accounts to control access to your computer. This means that different users have different privileges according to their account type.

Windows 10 Family Feature

This section briefly discusses different types of accounts you can create in Windows 10.

Administrator Account

Administrator accounts are accounts with all privileges and full-control. Administrator account holders can access all files and folders on the system by default. They can install new software, hardware, set up and delete additional accounts and do almost any operation on the computer. There is at least one administrator account by default.

Adult Account

When sharing your computer, you may add accounts for other members of your family as an administrator, so they can also use the computer and enjoy a personalized experience. In Windows 10, you can add an adult account and a child account.

Adding an adult account, as the name indicates is an account for responsible members of your family. An adult account can have the privileges of standard user, or of an administrator. A standard user may use the computer with full capabilities, however, they will not be able to install or uninstall software, or make changes to the PC which might affect other users (such as adding or deleting accounts or promoting a standard User Account to an administrator). They also have access to only a limited set of files.

When you create a new Adult account, it defaults to standard user.

Child Account

Microsoft introduces family features in Windows 10 which aims to provide a secure and pleasant online experience for kids. In Windows 10, you can also add accounts for all of the children in your family. Family features on Windows 10 allow you to set limits and permissions to the content children can access via the web browser. You can also configure activity reporting to monitor your children and know which websites they visit and the keywords they searched for, and the total time spent on each app/game on the PC. Additionally, you can restrict certain apps and games. Needless to say, a child's account cannot install or uninstall software or make changes that might affect other users on the PC. You can also set up a picture password for children who are too young to type a password.

All these activities can be monitored via the Microsoft online dashboard i.e. remotely, via the internet.

Setting up Multiple Accounts

Creating a Microsoft Account

To create a Microsoft User Account, follow these steps:

1- From the Start Menu Go to **Settings**.
2- Select **Accounts**.
3- Select **Family & Other** users from the left-side menu. You can create an account for your family members and individuals, giving them access to login to your PC.
4- Click on **+Add someone else to this PC** in *Other users*. Enter the Microsoft account of the member you want to add. Click Next. You are all set!

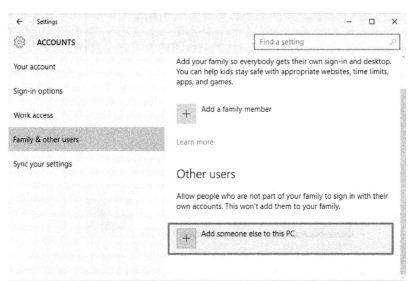

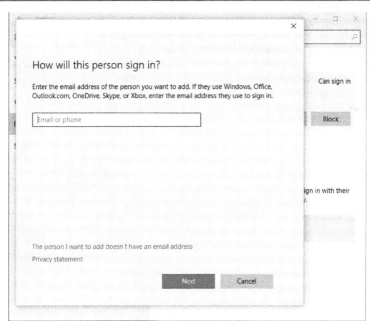

Good to go!

To log in the first time, [email address]90@hotmail.com will need to be connected to the internet.

Can sign in

Block

ign in with their

Finish

Creating Local Account

1- From Start Menu Go to **Settings**.
2- Select **Accounts**.
3- Select **Family & Other** users from the left-side menu. You can create account for your family members and individuals giving them access to login to your PC.
4- Click on **+Add someone else to this PC** in *Other users*
5- If you want to create a local account for a person then click on ***The person I want to add doesn't have an email address*** option on the bottom of the window. This will open another window offering you to create a Microsoft account. Identify the option *Add a user without a Microsoft account.* Add details i.e. username and password for the local account.

×

How will this person sign in?

Enter the email address of the person you want to add. If they use Windows, Office, Outlook.com, OneDrive, Skype, or Xbox, enter the email address they use to sign in.

Email or phone

The person I want to add doesn't have an email address

Privacy statement

| Next | | Cancel |

×

Let's create your account

Windows, Office, Outlook.com, OneDrive, Skype, Xbox. They're all better and more personal when you sign in with your Microsoft account.* Learn more

First name	Last name

someone@example.com

Get a new email address

Password

| United States | ∨ |

| Birth month | ∨ | Day | ∨ | Year | ∨ |

*If you already use a Microsoft service, go Back to sign in with that account.

Add a user without a Microsoft account

| Next | | Back |

Setting up Family Features

Windows 10 family features are only available for Family members. If you wish to create a User Account for your child and monitor his/her activity on your PC, then you will have to add your child as a member of your family. See detailed steps below:

1- Create a Microsoft email address for your child (with services such as Outlook, Hotmail etc.)
2- Add your child's email to your family list. You can do this my going to **Settings-> Accounts->Family & Other** and adding member to *your family* Section.
3- Microsoft will send an invite to your child's email address. Log in and accept the invitation.

You can then monitor your child's activity, set restrictions and use other family features.

Removing Accounts

An administrator can remove other User Accounts to deny access to their PC. To remove an account, follow these steps:

1- From the Start Menu Go to **Settings**.
2- Select **Account**.
3- Select **Family & Other** users from the left-side menu.
4- From the **Other users** section, select the user you want to remove. Click on the user to select it.

5- Click **Remove** to delete account.

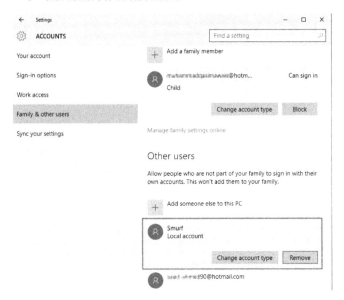

Chapter 17
SECURING YOUR SYSTEM WITH WINDOWS DEFENDER

With the PC and the Internet, comes security threats. With Windows 10 you have less to worry about when it comes to security! Thanks to the built-in anti-virus/anti malware feature known as **Windows Defender**. Windows Defender runs in the background and performs real-time scans to detect any malicious software running on the system. By default Windows Defender is turned on.

 Microsoft Security Essentials, free antivirus software by Microsoft offered in Windows 7 has been renamed as Windows Defender. Windows Defender is now built-into Windows 10. Both of them are essentially the same products and aim to provide a basic level of protection against malwares

Scan & Notifications

Windows Defender runs in background and performs regular scans to detect malware on your system. Whenever you download a file from the internet, access a file to open it and before you run a program, Windows Defender runs a scan to make sure the files are secure and safe to run.

Perhaps the best part is that Windows Defender is intended for everyday computer users with little or no knowledge of malware. Therefore when a threat is detected the anti-virus software takes appropriate action and does not require your intervention. If any threats are found, Windows Defender notifies you through the Action Center and through pop-up notifications. In the following figure you can see that Windows blocked potential malware when I attempted to download it.

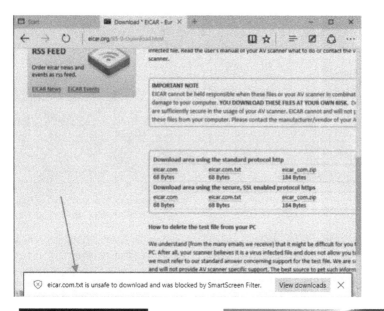

Windows Defender Settings

Windows Defender settings are integrated in the Windows Settings app. Windows Defender configuration settings in the Settings app are very simplified and you have minimum options to play around with or to learn. Therefore there is less chance to get things wrong and harm your PC. To access Windows Defender settings:

1- Open the **Start Menu** from the Start Button
2- Go to **Settings** App
3- Go to **Update & Security** and Select **Windows Defender** from the left menu.

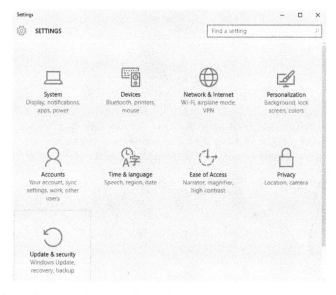

By default the Windows Defender is turned on and will scan items on your computer in real time. If you turn it off, let's say for a performance boost, Windows will turn Windows Defender on, automatically after a while to provide security.

Cloud based Protection and Sample submission allows Windows Defender to share security threat related information with Microsoft, with the aim to improve the software and to strengthen protection. Note that these are merely settings for Windows Defender. This is not the actual anti-virus software.

Manual Scan

If you come across a suspicious file/folder or device and need to examine it for potential malware, you can run manual scans. To run manual scan follow these steps:

1- Open the **Start Menu** from the Start Button
2- Go to **Settings** App
3- Go to **Update & Security** and Select **Windows Defender** from the left menu.
4- Scroll to the bottom of the window and click the option labeled, **Use Windows Defender.** This opens the anti-virus software. From here you can manually scan your computer, view and remove/restore infected files etc.

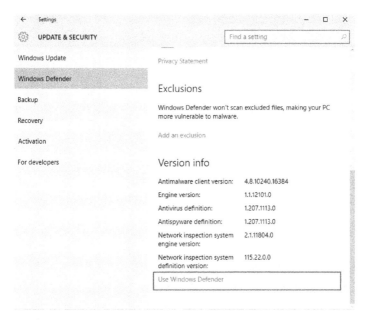

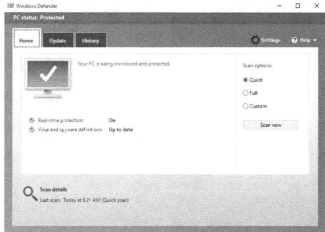

Viewing and Removing Detected Files

Windows Defender notifies you when it detects malware. You can view these malware files from within the Windows Defender anti-virus software. You may permanently remove the infected file or you may allow it to run (restore) only if you are sure that infected file is a false alarm. To view detected malware:

1- In the Windows Defender software, click to open History Tab.
2- Click the radio button besides **All detected items**, and click **View all** to view the list of infected files detected by Windows Defender.
3- Click on the checkbox to select an individual file. You may now remove it by clicking on the **Remove all** button, or simply **Allow item** (if you are sure that the file is *false positive*). For the purpose of demonstration, I have used fake malware files; these files are not actual virus/malware but are test files to check the functionality of the anti-virus software.

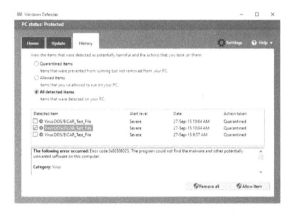

Updates

As new malwares are created, Anti-virus software needs to be updated to include more virus definitions so that they can block malicious software and protect you. Windows updates include the latest virus definitions for Windows Defender, therefore you do not manually need to update your antivirus software.

⚙ **VIEW YOUR UPDATE HISTORY**

Uninstall updates

Uninstall latest preview build

Update history

Definition Update for Windows Defender - KB2267602 (Definition 1.207.1113.0)
Successfully installed on 26-Sep-15

Definition Update for Windows Defender - KB2267602 (Definition 1.207.1108.0)
Successfully installed on 26-Sep-15

Definition Update for Windows Defender - KB2267602 (Definition 1.207.973.0)
Successfully installed on 25-Sep-15

Definition Update for Windows Defender - KB2267602 (Definition 1.207.757.0)
Successfully installed on 23-Sep-15

Technology is inherently unreliable. To say that your hard drive might crash one day and you could lose all your data wouldn't be an overly dramatic forethought. Therefore it's important to copy your data and save it to an alternative location. This practice is called creating a backup. Windows 10 includes a bunch of tools which will help you to protect your data and recover your important files in case of a system crash.

Windows 10 Backup Tools

Below is an overview of selected tools available for performing a system backup in Windows 10:

File History: Backup files are located in User Account libraries. We have already seen that libraries can display content from multiple folders. To create a file-history from libraries, you will have to add required folders to your library and show them in the File Explorer (discussed in chapter 8). Once you have added folders to specific libraries, Windows will automatically create a backup on another drive. When restoring, you are able to recover complete libraries or even a single file. This option is available in the **Settings** app as well as in Control Panel. The File History tool is perhaps the best tool to backup your pictures, files, music etc.

Backup & Restore Windows 7: The backup and restore feature which went missing in Windows 8 is now available in Windows 10. You can use this feature to create a complete backup of everything located on your hard-disk. Windows will also schedule a back-up (provided the external drive on which you have created or stored the data is plugged in) to update, backup and add any files which you have created recently.

System Image Backup: Creating a system image is like creating a one-time backup of your entire system. All data, including apps, system preferences and files and folders on your system at that point of time will be backed up. You can save this image of your file on an external drive and use this drive to recover your system to that state. This option is available in the Backup and Restore (Windows 7) tool. The System image is a complete copy of your entire system.

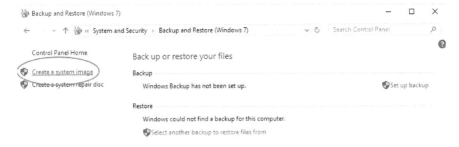

Reset this PC: This option reinstalls Windows. You can choose this option if you want to retain your files or delete them, which ever you prefer. We will discuss resetting Windows later in this chapter.

Backup & Restore Windows 7

Before you back up your data make sure:

1- Your external drive is plugged in. This is where Windows will save a copy of your data.
2- For best results, your external drive must be blank.
3- Your external drive must be formatted for the NTFS file system.

To backup your system using the Windows 7 backup tool, follow these steps:

1- Open Control Panel: Right-click on the start button and select Control Panel from the context menu.
2- Open **Backup and Restore (Windows 7)** in **System and Security** Section.
3- Identify **Set up backup** option under Back up or restore your files- Backup.
4- Select the Drive on which you want to create the Backup and click **Next**
5- Windows will create a backup on the selected drive. Back up will take time to finish, depending upon the quantity of data on your system. Once the backup is created you can

schedule the backup and Windows will automatically run the backup and update files. By default it is set to backup every week.

Restoring your Backup

To restore from a backup on your repaired computer one option would be to start with a fresh installation of Windows 10 from the original installation USB.

1- Plug-in the external drive on which you have created the backup.
2- When you start the Installation of Windows 10 (on your new or repaired computer) choose "Repair your computer", instead of the install option on the bottom of the screen.
3- Choose an Option -> **Troubleshoot**
4- Select Advanced Options->System Image Recovery: This will install Windows 10 using the system image on the backup drive. This will restore all your files and folders, including system preferences.
5- Select the system image you want to recover, click Next and follow the prompts.

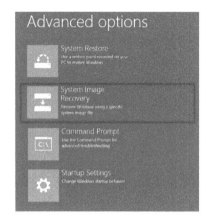

Reset Windows

Resetting Windows is the process of installing a fresh clean copy of Windows. Windows will handle the reinstallation process and will not require the installation drive. When resetting Windows you have two options:

1- **Keep Files:** If you select this option when resetting, all your files and User Accounts will be preserved. However any applications which you have installed on your system, whether they be from the Windows App Store or from the web or disks, will all be removed. This option is particularly handy if you have accidently installed malware and you are unable to remove it; or when an app is causing an issues in your system. Resetting will give you a fresh clean install of Windows with your files, which will help your system to run smoother and faster- though you will have to re-download and reinstall any and all apps.
2- **Remove Everything:** This option will remove everything from your PC; from apps to files, everything will be removed and you will get a fresh clean PC, just as it was when it was new!

To reset the computer follow these steps:

1- From Start Menu open the **Settings** app.
2- Open **Upgrade & Security**
3- Click on **Recovery**
4- Click on **Get Started** under Reset this **PC**

Resetting might take some time depending on the amount of data and apps you have stored on your PC.

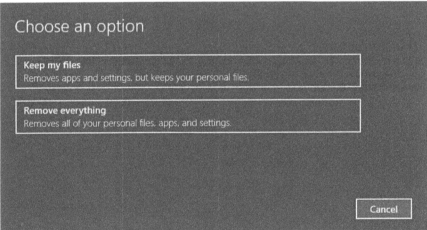

← Settings   − ☐ ✕

⚙ **UPDATE & SECURITY**   Find a setting   ⌕

Windows Update

Windows Defender

Backup

Recovery

Activation

For developers

Reset this PC

If your PC isn't running well, resetting it might help. This lets you choose to keep your files or remove them, and then reinstalls Windows.

Get started

Go back to Windows 7

This option is only available for a month after you upgrade to Windows 10.

Get started

Advanced startup

Start up from a device or disc (such as a USB drive or DVD), change Windows startup settings, or restore Windows from a system image. This will restart your PC.

Choose an option

Keep my files
Removes apps and settings, but keeps your personal files.

Remove everything
Removes all of your personal files, apps, and settings.

Cancel

You can also revert back to Windows 7 if you have upgraded your PC. However this is only possible within one month of the initial upgrade. After one month you will not be able to rollback your upgrade.

www.ingramcontent.com/pod-product-compliance
Lightning Source LLC
Chambersburg PA
CBHW071115050326
40690CB00008B/1234